People Are Talking

The principles and practices taught by the ServiceQuest book have positively affected the businesses and lives of business owners and entrepreneurs. The following testimonials are just a few of many examples. You may contact these people by emailing us at support@servicequest.com.

We are a Fortune 500 company exploring MLM [multi-level marketing] for one of our divisions. Your system and coaching have been amazing in every way; you have given us the confidence to proceed with our plan and the tools to get quickly into the market.

— DIEGO JIMINEZ

The launch system is much more than I had imagined. From strategies to forecasting, compensation design to staff training, you have saved us immeasurable amounts of time and money.

— RYAN BRICKNELL

You guys have given me the tools, contacts, guidance, and knowledge to turn my business from concept to reality. I really appreciate your support, and I look forward to taking this journey with you both by my side.

— MICHAEL FALLQUIST

The ServiceQuest team provides concrete, easy-to-follow advice that gives new direct sales companies specific advice and useful tools needed to plan, launch, and implement a business that is built for success. I look forward to a long-lasting relationship with ServiceQuest as we continue to grow and evolve.

— DIANNE PRINCE JOHNSTON

Your launch system has made all the difference for me. The executive training has been incredibly helpful, and the tools and templates really helped me to work through so many things that have to be done. I can't stop complimenting you on such a great system.

— VERONICA KASHLINKSY

Terrel Transtrum possesses the heart and vision of true customer service!

— FRANK VANDERSLOOT

The launch system has efficacy and integrity. Implementing the program results in savings and profits that quickly exceed costs. Every company should follow the principles offered by this highly respected organization.

— JEFFERY BABENER

You are exactly who I have been looking for because we need to launch at a hyper pace. Thanks for all your help.

— BLAKE REYNOLDS

You have given us the strategies and tools to keep up with our double-digit growth.

— JOHN EASTERLING

This book and the launch system present a truly exceptional foundation for a direct selling business. It's a complete guide for developing processes, mentoring key people, and building a $100 million direct selling enterprise. ServiceQuest is best in class.

— DAN JENSEN

I can't tell you how grateful I am and what a success our launch journey has been. Your thoughtful and thorough training and support have ensured our successful launch. The best practices, tools, and support prepared us for our growth. We look forward to continuing our journey with you.

— GARY CHARBONNEAU

As my personal mentor and the senior advisor to LuLaRoe, Terrel guided us from startup to $1.3 billion in 46 months. He is truly the best in the world.

— MARK STIDHAM

Terrel & Craig and the entire ServiceQuest organization are deeply dedicated to the successful launch and operation of each client. They are tireless and relentless, real success warriors.

— JASON HANSEN

People Are Talking

The principles and practices taught by the ServiceQuest team and this book have positively affected the businesses and lives of business owners and entrepreneurs. The following testimonials are just a few of many examples. You may contact these people by emailing us at support@ servicequest.com.

We are a Fortune 500 company exploring MLM [multi-level marketing] for one of our divisions. Your system and coaching have been amazing in every way; you have given us the confidence to proceed with our plan and the tools to get quickly into the market.

— DIEGO JIMINEZ

The launch system is much more than I had imagined. From strategies to fore-casting, compensation design to staff training, you have saved us immeasurable amounts of time and money.

— RYAN BRICKNELL

You guys have given me the tools, contacts, guidance, and knowledge to turn my business from concept to reality. I really appreciate your support, and I look forward to taking this journey with you both by my side.

— MICHAEL FALLQUIST

The ServiceQuest team provides concrete, easy-to-follow advice that gives new direct sales companies specific advice and useful tools needed to plan, launch, and implement a business that is built for success. I look forward to a long-lasting relationship with ServiceQuest as we continue to grow and evolve.

— DIANNE PRINCE JOHNSTON

Your launch system has made all the difference for me. The executive training has been incredibly helpful, and the tools and templates really helped me to work through so many things that have to be done. I can't stop complimenting you on such a great system.

— VERONICA KASHLINKSY

Terrel Transtrum possesses the heart and vision of true customer service!

— FRANK VANDERSLOOT

The launch system has efficacy and integrity. Implementing the program results in savings and profits that quickly exceed costs. Every company should follow the principles offered by this highly respected organization.

— JEFFERY BABENER

You are exactly who I have been looking for because we need to launch at a hyper pace. Thanks for all your help.

— BLAKE REYNOLDS

You have given us the strategies and tools to keep up with our double-digit growth.

— JOHN EASTERLING

This book and the launch system present a truly exceptional foundation for a direct selling business. It's a complete guide for developing processes, mentoring key people, and building a $100 million direct selling enterprise. ServiceQuest is best in class.

— DAN JENSEN

I can't tell you how grateful I am and what a success our launch journey has been. Your thoughtful and thorough training and support have ensured our successful launch. The best practices, tools, and support prepared us for our growth. We look forward to continuing our journey with you.

— GARY CHARBONNEAU

As my personal mentor and the senior advisor to LuLaRoe, Terrel guided us from startup to $1.3 billion in 46 months. He is truly the best in the world.

— MARK STIDHAM

Terrel & Craig and the entire ServiceQuest organization are deeply dedicated to the successful launch and operation of each client. They are tireless and relentless, real success warriors.

— JASON HANSEN

LAUNCH SMART!

LAUNCH SMART!

How to Build a Direct Sales Company

By **Terrel Transtrum** with **Craig A. Fleming**

Hearts & Smarts
PUBLISHING

Hearts & Smarts Publishing, PO Box 1742, Idaho Falls, ID 83403

10 9 8 7 6 5 4 3 2 1

ISBN 978-0-9906260-1-5 paperback

ISBN 978-0-9906260-2-2 ebook

Library of Congress

Launch Smart!: A Start-up Guide to Starting & Running a Successful Network Marketing & Party Plan Business / by Terrel Transtrum

1. Entrepreneurship. 2. Success in business. 3. New business enterprises.

I. Title. II. Launch Smart!: A Start-up Guide to Starting & Running a Successful

Network Marketing & Party Plan Business. III. Transtrum, Terrel

Library of Congress Control Number: 2014946519

www.servicequest.com
www.launchsmart.com

To business owners, executives, and entrepreneurs everywhere—the tenacious men and women who get up in the morning and make things happen—you make the world go round.

Table of Contents

Acknowledgements

We are deeply grateful to many who have helped us throughout the years in our research, teaching, coaching, mentoring, testing, and learning.

To our families, thank you for the love and support that changes, inspires, and enables us. Thank you particularly for your sacrifices and patience when we are far from home—or at home but overly focused our heads down over our keyboards and phones.

Thank you to our colleagues, associates, and team members who help in hundreds of ways—working to achieve our mission, serving our clients, training and coaching in ways that build a better world, and supporting one another with care, loyalty, and competence.

To our clients who trust us with their dreams as we go through the rigor of change and progress together, thank you.

To Britt Raybould, JT Eskelsen, and Jessie Lyon, thank you. Truly.

We owe a tremendous thanks to English professor and scholar Steve Stewart at BYU-Idaho for providing us with access to the senior English class for editing and refinements and to content/copy editor Addie Collett for sharing her gifts to turn these ideas from a can of nuts and bolts to a fine-tuned machine.

We believe we are all created to do something significant with our lives. Inside each is the spark of individual creativity that flows from agency—the right (and responsibility) to make good choices, to pursue ever-better courses, and to serve well. Those named and unnamed who contributed to this book live in a world of abundance, not in a world of scarcity, and are making a difference by living significantly.

Overview

Although some people call direct selling an *industry*, we prefer to think of it as a marketing channel that delivers products directly to consumers through independent representatives. It is not necessary to refer to this business model as *network marketing* or *party plan* in order to take full advantage of the powerful elements they contain. You as the business owner decides which selling methods work best for your company.

This start-up guide has been created for:

- Entrepreneurs considering launching a new direct selling start-up company
- Owners of an existing business that may benefit from a direct selling division or change in marketing and sales strategies
- Executives of an existing direct selling business who are interested in taking their business to the next level

The goal in presenting this start-up guide is to provide you with a reliable tool to start the planning process. Since 1988, we have mentored hundreds of direct selling companies in best practices, and we have found that a company is better off using this start-up guide than completely "winging it." With a small investment, a company might take the next step and invest in our system and advisory support.[1] This will make the journey even more agreeable since it will increase the likelihood of success by removing guesswork and minimizing risks. We want you to have the secrets to success at the beginning of your journey, not at the middle or the end.

In this start-up guide, we provide you with principles and key concepts for starting and running a successful direct selling company. Each chapter contain important information and checklists of essential action steps for launching. These action steps correspond with our optional workshops and workbooks that will give you all you need to know to launch your direct selling company. If you choose to jump in

---

1   Our team has created a system called LaunchSmart which is a comprehensive system with supporting methodologies for taking the best practices of our large clients and bundling them for concise and efficient learning and implementation.

on starting your business without these resources, the checklists in this book will provide you with a place to start. In addition, in the Appendix, we provide you with lists of other resources available to you.

Use this guide to capture your thoughts, questions, commitments, notes, and goals. Throughout this guide, we provide you with activities, examples, and questions to consider to help you in this process. Should you find yourself struggling or in need of encouragement, always remember that we're a phone call or email away. Additionally, our ServiceQuest team is always willing to help, no matter what stage of the game you're in.

Introduction
Foundational Learning

One of the best-kept secrets in the world is the direct selling model of marketing and distributing products. While not new, it is a method of distribution that few people understand. As you read this book, you will gain a better understanding of how you can successfully build a profitable direct selling business through best practices and sound principles.

Direct Selling

Direct selling is the sale of products or services directly to consumers without a permanent or fixed retail location. A company can grow quickly with a volunteer sales force of independent representatives[2]. In a direct selling business, the company and independent reps have various roles:

- The company's roles are to:
  - ☐ Provide products or services
  - ☐ Centralize fulfillment and operations to serve the entire organization
  - ☐ Develop compensation, awards, incentives, and programs to stimulate growth
  - ☐ Process commissions
  - ☐ Maintain genealogies
  - ☐ Administer policies and procedures
  - ☐ Support the field organization with trainings and events

---

2   Distributors is the most commonly used term for independent representatives in network marketing companies, and consultants seems to be the most common convention for home party plan companies. There are several other creative references that reflect the personality of the company such as affiliate and IBO (Independent Business Owner). For our purposes, we use independent representative (or "rep" as our shorthand) in this guide to depict the independent sales representative who sells products and recruits other sellers to their business organizations.

- [ ] Drive communications and provide customer service
- [ ] Capitalize start-up and financially support all aspects of growth
- [ ] Oversee development of products and services to meet market demands
- [ ] Monitor compensation and incentives for flaws
- The independent reps' roles are to:
  - [ ] Sell products and services provided by the company
  - [ ] Create a base of customers and provide service and product training to them
  - [ ] Develop and manage an organization of people who recruit and sell
  - [ ] Train, inspire, and lead those in their sales organizations
  - [ ] Learn and apply the methodologies and systems promoted by the company

Network Marketing and Party Plan

Over the years, direct selling has primarily consisted of two distinct models: the party plan and the network marketing[3]. Each has a sales force comprised of independent representatives that earn commissions and bonuses from selling products.

Both types of companies feature multi-level compensation of one type or another. It is a framework through which sale percentages flow based on predetermined qualifications and is paid based on the independent rep's level. The representatives are attracted by the opportunity to get compensation—not only on their personal sales but also on the sale volumes of others in various levels of their sales organization. Much like traditional sales organizations, multi-level compensation exists as incentives for the small percentage of skilled, driven, and visionary leaders who get out of bed each day to get the job done.

The differences in the two models begin to appear in a spectrum of product selling methodology, ranging from a retail foundation (where products are discounted to the seller who in turn raises the price to make a profit) to the consumption model (where a product that is consumed consistently is sold).

---

3   Network marketing is also commonly known as multi-level marketing (MLM).

Network marketing companies are designed for one-to-one selling and can sometimes be identified by their more complex compensation plans. These companies typically consider each active account worth one hundred dollars per month in sales on average. However, they often incorrectly classify all accounts as independent representatives, when the majority are actually customer accounts.

Party plan companies are designed to support social gatherings by targeting groups of people who have common interests or who come to support a friend hosting the gathering in exchange for free products and discounts. In 2018, the Direct Selling Association (DSA) reported that the average home party consisted of eight orders averaging $54 per order, or roughly $432 in sales per party. Some companies report home parties that generated as much as $800 to $1,000 or more per party.

Both types of companies are successful when they focus their efforts on finding and developing customers. It may be tempting to view the prize as being builders or being the one to convince the most people to sign up, but the reality is that the company that focuses on delivering genuine value to customers will have the most success.

Activity: Network Marketing & Party Plan

Considering the fundamental differences between network marketing and party plan models, which type of model best supports your company's objectives?

- Network marketing
- Party plan
- Hybrid
- Not sure

Describe how you envision using the internet for your direct selling business.

List qualities and features of direct selling companies that you plan to incorporate into your company.

Web Marketing

Web marketing has become an integral part of direct selling. The greatest caution we extend is to never forget that direct selling is person-to-person selling and that there are certain tasks that cannot be done through an electronic medium.

The most powerful use of the internet we have experienced is in the ServiceQuest® OPSY Viral Ops™. This system combines cutting-edge web marketing that funnels, searches, and recruits at the most basic level of human behavior.

Start-up in 180 Days or Less

Can you really start and run a successful direct selling company in 180 days or less? Yes, you can. The world has changed dramatically in recent years. Today, we can use online tools to do things much faster than was possible a few years ago. When you look at the core elements of a new direct selling business, the actual tasks involved don't take that much time. Technically, it takes about an hour to register a name for your business and to become a legal entity. Setting up a location can take a couple of hours if it's in your home or as little as a few days if it's in an office somewhere near where you live.

It's true that not all businesses can go straight from the first spark of an idea to the full and complete execution in just 26 weeks, but many can. It all depends on your experience and your learning curve. It's also true that the essence of a direct selling company doesn't just scale and grow; however, since it's a cash-up-front business, it usually sustains its own growth.

Pilots and Test Parties

Testing your ideas and business model may be the most important (and most overlooked) step in the launch process. Some companies (especially party plan companies) conduct pilots or test parties before launching their direct selling businesses.

Pilots and test parties can provide answers to these important questions:

- Will guests buy your products at home parties?
- How much will the average guest spend on products and services?
- How much will the average party generate in sales?
- How much will hosts spend?
- What percentage of guests will host a party of their own?
- What percentage of guests will be interested in becoming a rep?
- Is the host rewards program configured correctly for your business?
- Does the sales presentation script work well?
- What do guests like best about your home parties?
- What can you do to make the parties more enjoyable and more successful?

As you collect information from each test party, you will gain valuable information that you can use for setting commission percentages on personal sales, expectations and dollar-per-hour earnings in the compensation plan, and specifics of the host rewards program.

The test party outline included in our workshop guides you through which decisions need to be made, which tasks need to be performed, which materials need to be developed, and which responsibilities need to be assigned.

Customer and Representative Profiles

Generally, you will have two classes of clients: the customer and the independent representative. Understanding customers and reps is extremely crucial in direct selling.

The first class of client is the consumer. They will assess the value of the products and services based on the benefits (such as convenience and quality) they receive. If they do not receive value, they will stop buying.

The second class of client is the independent representatives. They will be a true customer as a consumer of the products and services. They will also be a customer of your business opportunity and all the training and support you offer. If they benefit from this relationship, they will stick with it. If they don't, they won't.

The more you know about the personal characteristics of customers and reps, the better you can meet their needs. This exercise becomes important since each customer or rep will join your company on their terms and timelines and with their own expectations. To help you get started, we have prepared a basic profile of the general characteristics of direct selling customers and reps. Customers and reps can be classified in a variety of ways, including:

- Personality types
- Place in life
- Hereditary factors
- Environmental factors

We believe that we are on solid ground if we stand on the Abraham Maslow model of human needs, with the premise that a company's purpose should be to create and foster a culture that attracts people who seek to be happy. Thus, the relevant question would be "what makes customers and reps happy?"

These classifications align with the "on-ramps" of customers and reps—where they are in their lives and what they want from the company. In other words, what is their "why" for taking the step to join the company?

Activity: Customer & Rep Profiles

Get an idea of the kind of people who will use your product and why. Make a list of the following:

- People who will buy your products and services
- Reasons people will purchase your products and services
- People who will become independent representatives for your company
- Reasons people will become reps for your company
- Special training or licenses you will require before accepting a new recruit

Customers

These are the profiles of customers who order either from an independent representative or directly from the company because of their contact with a rep (for example, they may order from the rep's company-linked website).

 Loyal Lola is the kind of person who loves and supports the independent representative. She can usually be counted on for long-term support as long as she is kept updated and continues to be thanked and encouraged. It is also good to show her how her support benefits the rep who is trying to be a responsible breadwinner for his or her family. Loyal Lola likes party plan sales better than network marketing because she only has to purchase periodically (whenever their independent rep has a party or new catalog) rather than committing to buying monthly.

 Healthy Hank is the enthusiast looking for the specific benefits that the product or service offers. He sees sufficient value in that product or service to justify the ongoing purchases and pays no attention initially to the business opportunities. He understands how to spot the features and knows what benefits he is seeking. However, a well-told story about the company's efforts to sustain value from a rep is usually sufficient to spark his interest and sustain his ongoing purchasing and consumption behaviors.

 ADHD Andy is an impulsive buyer who loves bright and flashy things. He often grabs onto every new fad that goes by, until the next bright and flashy thing comes along. He, however, is in the minority.

Independent Representatives

Representatives of a direct selling company who earn income through retail sales, overrides, commissions, incentives, promotions, contests, and all mixes of these are independent-business builders. They are contracted independent representatives who comprise the volunteer sales force of direct selling companies. These are the men and women who get out of their beds in the morning and decide to make something happen.

Easy Earl is the optimistic customer who sees being a rep as a money-making opportunity. He has no real intention of working the business, is afraid of selling, and breaks out in night sweats at the thought of telling someone about his new venture. Nevertheless, he holds out for the possibility, however remote, that he might hit the jackpot in some way. He is likely to jump into the "get rich quick!" line. This mentality fuels ongoing activity until he discovers or resolves that there is no longer a reason to believe.

 Happy Hannah knows a few people who would buy the products, resulting in some small bonuses or commissions. She doesn't give much thought to what's beyond and leaves open the possibility that she could get invited to a meeting or gathering that will inspire her further. If the invitation doesn't come, the emotional juice burns off, and she fades into the customer profiles, or possibly into obscurity, never to be heard of again. Happy Hannah loves a get-together and wants everybody to be happy.

 Busy Betty is a stay-at-home mom who has a baby in her lap and one under the desk as she is searching for a home-based business opportunity to help earn extra monthly income to help cover family shortfalls and to have a little of her own spending money. She is smart and intuitive. Busy Betty will find something that works for her and is motivated to pick up the phone and get things moving with her neighbors, friends, and family members. She has a small circle of friends and acquaintances that she will contact via phone, social media, and email and in-person.

 Hard-working Harry is determined to at least earn a few thousand in hopes he can change his lifestyle or possibly even transition into career-level income. He thinks $500 to $1,000 is okay for starters but finds himself going through steep learning curves and soon becomes frustrated by his lack of experience or training. Still, he doesn't lose heart and begins to make more money than he spends on products. He reasons that his custom-ers will never stop buying products and that he will always meet the minimum requirements to receive commissions. He may be sitting on the fence between part-time and career and will slide into the middle ground until something big blasts him to the next level. He is often in the category of leaders who find themselves an "accidental leader," unsure how he got to advanced levels.

 Career Cathy is a seasoned, savvy, and visionary direct seller with experience and training in sales. She comes from a place of sheer vision and determination. She knows how to make a prospecting list, contact and qualify, plant seeds, invite, close sales, build a following, support customers, and inspire support. Regardless of where she learned these skills, she has ambitions to earn six-figures from her efforts as a rep, and nothing will stop her.

Ongoing Learning

The power of applying key business fundamentals to successfully launch and run your direct selling company is best experienced in real time with real situations in your real world. To provide you with an inspiring big-picture view and a taste of immediate results even before you have your own experiences, we have organized this book in a linear format that puts the essence of this dynamic art of workflow management and personal productivity into perspective.

Our LaunchSmart™ system is also a resource to help you with your ongoing learning. With our system, we provide you with training that contributes to key launch decisions, workshops and prelaunch support, and continued support through launch and beyond.

Your Network of Trusted Advisors

As you seek out advice on your business, you will likely talk with trusted advisors and friends. Your trusted advisors and friends can refer you to other direct selling professionals, and you may discover more through your research and networking efforts.

Identify the issues that experienced direct selling professionals can assist with. Find those who are dedicated to teaching you the best principles and practices so that you can make sense of the different aspects of network and party plan marketing.

Stages of Business Development

If you have completed the LaunchSmart™ Day 1 Advantage™ system, you will have a good idea of where you are in your business development path. If not, we provide here a summary of the general stages.

Idea Stage

The idea stage is where all creation begins, whether the idea is a solution to a problem or an avenue for something better, no matter how great or small. Author and thought leader, Napoleon Hill, taught, "All achievements, all earned riches, have their beginning in an idea." The true role of a successful leader in a direct selling enterprise is to inspire reps and builders to dream and then to motivate them to act.

If an idea has been in the back (or front) of your mind, examine that idea. If it is questionable whether the idea is something that you can be best in the world at and deeply passionate about, then the idea should be challenged and refined and even abandoned if it does not inspire you.

Creation Stage

If you have begun the creation process of forming your business, you should be facing questions as you move along. You may not have all the answers, and even more importantly, you may not know all the questions to ask. These self-assessment questions can help you in this stage:

- Are you writing a business plan?
- Does your business plan include an itemized budget?
- Have you determined all the tasks to be performed to launch?
- Have you assigned people to tasks?
- Are your project plan and timeline in place?
- Have you determined the skills of those on your team?
- Have you selected the products or services that you plan to sell?
- Is your compensation plan completed, and does it line up with the five key behaviors?
- Are incentives in place to attract initial recruits?
- Is the rep career plan fully defined?

This self-assessment opens the doors to more detailed questions and assessments that will follow in subsequent stages of our workshop. The importance of these questions is to frame your mind for receiving the guidance and instruction that follows.

Perplexed Stage

If you are already launched and some things are going well for you, but others are not, you are probably feeling the effects of having some missing elements in your business. The good news is your feelings can be one of the best tools in bringing about further exploration and action. Business is not an exact science, but the best businesses take their best actions, evaluate results, adjust the course, and continue forward.

For instance, you may have a base of reps who are selling products and recruiting customers and other reps. You would like to see the business grow faster. It may be time for you to examine the company's role in recruiting. You may have discovered that your trusted employees aren't performing at the level of your expectations. It's probably time to evaluate skills and attitudes, match them up to the staffing plan, and evaluate the allocation of assignments and responsibilities.

If you are in the Perplexed Stage, consider these questions:

- Did you write a complete business plan?
- Has the business plan been updated to reflect changes in the company?
- Are you using an itemized budget to manage your business?
- Have you assigned the right tasks to the right resources?
- Have you taken time to evaluate skills and attitudes of all team members?
- Have you been following trends and responding in the best ways?
- Are you using technology to improve the customer/rep experience?
- Are you using systems that provide you with the right information for guiding the business?
- Is the compensation plan producing the right results?
- Do incentives work as intended?

- Is your company genuinely pursuing the success and happiness of its reps?

Transition Stage

If you are an established company with a retail or wholesale business, you may be exploring growth options through direct selling avenues, either a complete conversion or the launch of a direct selling division.

A growing number of ServiceQuest clients have observed the successes of direct selling models and have decided to explore direct selling as a new channel for their business. While there are many similarities in business, there are also important differences to consider when transitioning to direct selling.

If you are in this stage, consider these questions:

- Will you be selling the same products through direct selling channels?
- Do you have a strategy to manage channel conflicts?
- Will you use existing brands to promote direct selling?
- Do you have management support at all levels to enter direct selling?
- Do you have a business plan that addresses the direct selling initiative?
- Does the business plan include an itemized budget?
- Do you have realistic growth projections for the direct selling business?

Blended Stage

You may find yourself in a blended environment of more than one of these stages. Step back and consider where you are, how open you are to learn and apply new principles and concepts, and how capable you are of committing the energy and resources to forging ahead.

Conclusion

Now that we have established the foundation of what a direct selling business entails, you are almost ready to dive into preparing your business for launching. First, complete the list below of essential action steps for launching to set the foundation for the rest of your launch preparations.

Essential Actions for Launching

- ☐ Learn the foundations of successfully launching and running a direct selling business
- ☐ Commit to ongoing learning and development
- ☐ Establish your network of trusted advisors

Chapter 1
Strategy

Having a strategic plan for what your business will look like, how you will share it, and how you will grow it will be crucial to having a successful direct selling company. It will serve as the road map for every internal business decision you make. Starting it early will allow you to have a direction right from the beginning. Approach the task of making your plan with complete honesty, and carefully consider each question that arises in the process. With all of this in mind, your strategic plan should be reflected in the form of a "living" document: one that you will revisit, review, and update annually.

Your Strategic Vision Statement

Having an entrepreneurial dream is the first step toward creating your strategic plan and turning it into a reality. If you do it right, you can create a clear picture of what your company will be like when it's developed. You will describe this picture in your strategic vision statement. With this foundation, everything will move forward to build your business.

Contents of Your Strategic Vision Statement

Crafting a strategic vision statement is a creative task. You'll probably write and rewrite it many times until you are satisfied with it. It's best to do the writing in two steps. First, describe the company in general, and then add the unique elements that make it remarkable. The following activity can be used as a point of departure.

Activity: Basic Characteristics

Write out the basic characteristics of your business. Then write the unique characteristics your business has to offer. The following lists will provide you with ideas of what to write. Keep in mind that you may need to add or skip items on these lists depending on what applies to your vision.

- Basic Characteristics:
  - ☐ Line of business, products, services offered
  - ☐ Company size (sales, profits, employees)
  - ☐ Company growth (sales, production)
  - ☐ Geographic scope
  - ☐ Markets served
  - ☐ Timing, when the business will be "fully developed"
  - ☐ Basis of competition (price, quality, service, etc.)
- Unique Characteristics:
  - ☐ Unique products, services
  - ☐ Unique marketing
  - ☐ Compensation system
  - ☐ Unique "presence" (look, sound, feel)
  - ☐ Unique operations

Writing Your Strategic Vision Statement

Now that you have your entrepreneurial dream and a list of the general and unique characteristics of your business, you are ready to prepare your strategic vision statement. Be sure to make your statement clear and write it down. This will force you to think about the details of your vision and how you will communicate your vision to others. When you are done with writing your statement, it should be a page or less in length. To get an idea of what a strategic vision statement could look like, consider this example.

Example Strategic Vision Statement

This strategic vision statement models what home economics teacher Doris Christopher could have written when she was planning to launch her new company, The Pampered Chef, from her Illinois basement in 1980.

Within twenty years, The Pampered Chef will be a nationwide distributor of time-saving kitchen tools and techniques designed to make cooking quick and easy. Our professional-quality kitchen equipment will be offered directly to consumers through in-home cooking demonstrations performed by a sales force of Pampered Chef independent representatives. Customers will see how the products work, try them out, and even taste the results.

The company will become a member of the Direct Selling Association (DSA) and serve the direct selling profession with energy and passion. The company will progress into facilities and work environments that provide meaningful jobs and careers for local employees, while the sales and marketing channels will provide part-time and career opportunities for individuals throughout North America.

The company will exceed $700 million in sales and have more than 60,000 Pampered Chef independent representatives, many of whom are mothers who have been empowered to develop lucrative businesses while staying home to raise their children and manage their households.

The company will bring families together, not only through its direct selling opportunity but also through its product line. Each piece will be designed to make cooking faster and easier so that customers can spend less time in the kitchen and more time with their families. When families share a meal, the bonds that hold that family together grow stronger.

The company will maintain a simple business philosophy, supporting independent representatives and customers with world-class customer service. Employees will treat independent representatives and customers as friends by showing warmth, caring, and competence in their work.

Operations will follow exact procedures, emphasizing quality products delivered on time, accurate commissions paid on time, and caring service with consistency and follow-through.

In this example is successful in portraying the vision of The Pampered Chef because it highlights what makes it unique and what new services and opportunities it will bring to the market. It simply outlines the company and their plans to follow a direct selling model and then goes deeper by expressing what the company intends to achieve through specific goals.

It's easy to write a strategic vision after the fact, as we have done with The Pampered Chef example above. The genius lies in understanding your markets and your business opportunity before it actually happens. Create a vision that fits the opportunity, and then make it happen. Remember, it's not enough for you to have a vision. You have to use it. If you don't, it won't work.

Dynamic yet Stable

Your strategic vision should be dynamic and subject to revision when necessary. However, it should also be stable and not subject to change every time the wind blows. Think of it as your company's version of the U.S. Constitution. Preserve and regard it with a degree of reverence but be willing to make changes when needed.

Your Company Story

Your company story illustrates the core of what your business is all about. It is a tale of passion, motivation, opportunity, and love. Remember, big businesses started small and made the right choices. They created stories that built an understanding of the spirit of the company. Your company story illustrates what makes your business different from everyone else.

Looking at industry today, everything seems the same. Our nation is in a service crisis. The market is bored and so are employees and independent representatives. People need a place of community that has purpose, order, and meaning. Your business can become a place where words such as integrity, intention, commitment, vision, and excellence are used as action steps in producing a worthwhile result.

Your Tale to Tell

Your story can be about how your business started or what your business does. It could be like the inspiring story of Gene Hughes, a Utah schoolteacher who experienced a nagging stomach condition. Gene's story shows that the start of a good company can come from simple things and that you don't have to be an expert to start a good business.

Gene took the advice of a neighbor who suggested cayenne pepper for his discomfort, and it worked! Even though he felt much better, it was awful having to swallow a spoonful of cayenne pepper. His wife, Kristine, suggested putting the powder into easy-to-swallow gelatin capsules. The result was revolutionary. They soon enlisted the support of family to begin a small business selling encapsulated cayenne and other herbs to health food stores. Nature's Sunshine Products now operates in 33 countries and is represented by more than half a million independent representatives worldwide.

Your story may not be like Gene's. Yours could be about the dedicated employees who hold your business together through the toughest times, or it might be about someone going beyond his or her comfort zone to achieve an incredible result.

Being an entrepreneur is about branding your business as something exceptional in a market of mediocrity. What can you say about the birth of your business? What about its energy?

Think about the principles you believe in. What do you want in your business and your life to be genuine? How can you best illustrate that spirit? Think back through the years of history and find one incident that reflects that spirit. That is your story.

It's All About Inspiration

Company stories have an impact. Any great business has a reason for being that can touch its customers, employees, and independent representatives very deeply. That reason is what your company story is all about. It's the heart and soul of why you're in business.

Have fun with writing your story. Not every story needs to be lengthy. It just needs to be your story. It needs to be real. And it needs to be told.

Example: SendOutCards Company Story

Consider the story behind SendOutCards, a custom online greeting card system that's been around since 2003. Pay attention to how it's story reflects the desire to help others touch those around them through encouraging messages.

SendOutCards is about changing people's lives for good, one card at a time. We believe we can change the world, one card at a time. We are showing that we can create residual income, one card at a time.

Some of the greatest minds of the past century have been telling us the keys to success involve showing constant respect to others. Abraham Lincoln stated that "everybody likes a compliment." This is how he ran our country and became the greatest political leader of all time—he simply complimented people.

William James said, "The deepest principle in human nature is the craving to be appreciated." Notice the strong language he used. He said the "craving" to be appreciated.

I can already hear business-minded people saying, "Okay, this is all great, but what does this mean to my bottom line? How can I prosper financially by implementing these principles?" Let's answer that question with a true story:

In 1921, a man by the name of Charles Schwab was picked by Andrew Carnegie to become the first president of the United States Steel Company. Schwab's salary was $1 million per year. When asked why he was paid so much money, Schwab replied: "I was paid this salary largely because of my ability to deal with people."

When asked how he dealt with people, he said, "I consider my ability to arouse enthusiasm among my people the greatest asset I possess, and the way to develop the best that is in a person is appreciation and encouragement." Charles Schwab went on to become one of the greatest business leaders of all time.

Dale Carnegie said, "We nourish the bodies of our children and friends and employees, but how seldom do we nourish their self-esteem? We provide them with roast beef and potatoes to build energy, but we neglect to give them kind words of appreciation that would sing in their memories for years like the music of the morning stars."

When was the last time you told your son or daughter that you were proud of them? Or your employees that they did a great job? Or your husband or wife that you love him or her? Or your friend that you appreciate the friendship you share? Or your customers that you appreciate their business?

Remember, we as human beings crave appreciation. When we show it, people will respond to us in the most positive ways possible.

Everyone has promptings to do these things, but we seldom act on those promptings. The difference between success and failure in your life will depend on your ability to act on the promptings of sharing kind words or deeds.

Numerous studies in human development suggest it is easier to express ourselves in writing as opposed to audibly. SendOutCards gives you the tools to respond to your promptings instantly by expressing your appreciation in writing. And the best part? You can do it in seconds.

With today's technology, you can implement simple rules that will make a significant impact in your personal and professional life. You will be able to make a big difference for good in the lives of everyone you associate with.

SendOutCards doesn't just give a story about why their business is important, but they really integrate that story in people's personal day-to-day cares by showing how this issue has been addressed by successful people throughout history. Through their story, SendOutCards shows that the issue they are addressing matters.

Your Business Plan

A business plan is a document that summarizes the operational and financial objectives of your business. It contains detailed plans and budgets that show how your objectives are to be brought about. Your business plan will also help you describe your business in detail from a variety of perspectives—not only for funding but also for guiding your team.

The purpose of a business plan is to secure outside investment capital. However, the best plans have more to them than just this. They contain well-researched preparation combined with an energetic visionary who has a product or service that enough people will buy to make the business worthwhile.

For an example of a successful business plan's content, see Table 1–1 in the Appendix.

Your Growth and Financial Model

Our approach to forecasting growth and financial results is a two-pronged approach. The first prong is the expected builder behaviors model that are based on our years of observing and quantifying performance. A good forecast considers past performance, but it also looks forward with an eye on what's different now than in the past.

We have learned that people are people and that we can rely on some of their basic behaviors in creating our growth models. The growth model incorporated in our spreadsheets and software forecasting tools is driven by questions and assumptions such as "out of 100 active reps in the month of February, how many will make a business presentation?" and "of those making business presentations, how much will they make?" These lead to question such as "of business presentations (or home parties) conducted, how many recruits and how much in sales will result?" and so forth. These series of behavioral assumptions then drive the financial forecasts.

The second prong is financial forecasting. Typically, this prong is much more scientific than the expected behavioral model prong. The financial statements most commonly used by investors and executives in managing and planning business are the following:

- Profit and loss statement
- Balance sheet
- Cash flow statement

Interestingly, the one we find ourselves watching most carefully is the cash flow statement. It predicts of how much cash or credit we need access to at any given time in the company's growth cycle. It's the key to not outgrowing available resources, which is one of the primary causes of failure.

Marketing Strategies

Most direct selling, start-up companies enlist the support of a marketing firm. This firm will help you develop your company name, product or service name, logos, packaging, branding, sales tools, advertising strategies, websites, etc. This firm will be one of your most important strategic partners. You will find that the degree to which they can effectively help you will depend upon how ready you are to let them understand you, your products and services, and where you want to take your company.

We provide a planning system to prepare you to interact with your marketing firm. The information you generate using this planning system will evolve as you interact with your marketing firm, but it's vital that you take the first step in making the key decisions required herein. Don't forget—it's your company. If you choose not to use a marketing firm and create your own materials, using this planning system to organize your thoughts will be even more important. Our marketing strategy workshop is designed to help you succeed in creating the right marketing plan that merges with your direct selling business objectives.

Our basic marketing strategy workshop will be well worth the effort. In the workshop we will apply the concepts introduced here:

- **Basic Business Concept:** Describe your basic business concept. What business are you in? What is your primary mission? How will you make money?

- **Basic Product Concept:** Describe your basic product concept. What are the main products and/or services you will be selling? What are their specific features and benefits?

- **Branding:** What are your branding strategies, simple brand ideas, and branding signals?

- **Overall Market Description:** Describe the overall market you will be targeting (health care, home crafts and hobbies, skin care, etc.). Describe the market size, characteristics, and key trends.

- **Specific Market Segment Description:** Describe the specific market segment(s) you will be targeting (general wellness vitamins, energy drinks, scrap booking, anti-aging creams, etc.). Describe the market segment size, characteristics, and key trends.

- **Target Market Description:** Describe in detail the characteristics of those you will target to purchase your products and/or services (age, sex, ethnicity, income level, occupation, marital status, etc.). Write a profile for the users of each product and/or service.

- **Competitive Analysis:** Describe in detail the products and/or services that are currently being offered within your market segment to your target market. What are the key features and benefits of competitive offerings? What are their branding messages? Are there any features and benefits valued by your target market that are currently not being addressed by competitive offerings that yours could address?

- **Unique Selling Proposition:** Describe in detail your unique selling proposition. What will your customers and independent representatives really be buying from you, and why will they buy it from you rather than someone else? What makes you truly unique? How will you position your products and/or services in contrast to the competition? Complete this analysis for each product and/or service you will offer at launch.

- **General Awareness Marketing:** Describe the specific strategies you will use to create general market awareness for your product and/or service in the minds of your target market. What mediums will you use (billboards, magazines, websites, television, etc.)? Be sure to consider which avenues will best reach your specific target market. What will your key messages be?

- **Lead Generation Marketing Strategies:** Describe the specific strategies you will use to generate qualified leads for your independent representatives. These will be people who express an interest in your products and/or services. Use caution when considering purchasing leads. Be sure the characteristics of the leads match your specific target market characteristics. Make sure the leads have the correct contact information and you know how many times the leads you are buying have been sold to others. These strategies should be closely aligned with your general awareness marketing strategies above. Remember that one of the common barriers preventing growth of direct selling professionals is not knowing where to go for additional leads after exhausting their circle of warm contacts.

- **Independent Representative Specific Marketing:** Describe the specific strategies you will use to create awareness for your products or services in the minds of your independent representative target market. What mediums will you use (billboards, magazines, websites, television, radio, newspaper, public relations activities, etc.)? Be sure to consider those avenues that will best reach your specific target market.

- **Product Specific Marketing Strategies:** Describe any marketing strategies that are required for specific products or services that will not be part of your overall marketing strategy.

Remember, the goal of these strategies is to create awareness so that when your independent representatives contact prospective customers and reps, those prospects will already have a positive image of your products and/or services in their mind.

Launching Internationally

After viewing the tremendous international success of companies such as Avon, Nikken, Amway, NuSkin, Mary Kay, and Tupperware, many owners of start-up network marketing companies are tempted to go into international markets immediately. The short answer is don't do it.

Starting a successful network marketing company is a complex task—a process that should be perfected one step at a time. It is important to first develop a working model in the United States or country of origin.

Mastering the marketing plan, establishing independent representative and customer service departments, refining the support technology, etc. are best accomplished in one country. Duplication in foreign markets can follow once that machine is working.

In addition, it is important for independent reps to focus their efforts in one market rather than spreading their efforts across multiple markets ineffectively. Of course, all rules have exceptions, and if your company is a multi-billion-dollar corporation with worldwide retail stores or international catalog operations, you may have the resources available for a multi-country launch. For the smaller businesses, the best option is a logical progression from the United States to Canada, Europe, Australia, Asia, Mexico, and South America.

Many companies believe that the internet has made international expansion an instantaneous event. Unfortunately, the internet and technology are far ahead of the legal and business requirements of going international. For those who really wish to approach international markets in a rational business and legal manner, we have provided a summary of points from the article, "Network Marketing: Going International," which can be found, along with other resources, at www.mlmlegal.com.

Consider these points when looking into moving your business internationally:

- **Corporate and Foreign Lawyers:** Locate counsel in the foreign country that has expertise in direct selling. You may need to locate several different types of lawyers with expertise in direct sales, including food and drug, taxes, corporate structure. Include your usual corporate counsel in the loop as you move into foreign countries to create some continuity throughout the world system.

- **Trademarks:** Look into registering your company, product, and service trademarks as early as possible, preferably even before entry into the country. Companies are always surprised to find themselves being held hostage to well-meaning distributors or greedy pirates who have already registered important company trademarks.

- **Consumer Legislation:** Every country has variations on deceptive trade practices, laws, consumer laws, and anti-pyramiding statutes. These vary around the world, and you should check out the local pyramid scheme acts to make sure that your compensation plan and method of marketing are in tune. In fact, in many countries, you may be able to receive opinion letters, advisory opinions, or approvals by government agencies as to the marketing program before entry.

- **Earnings Claims:** Check out the sorts of restrictions that you and your independent reps may make with respect to the business opportunity you are offering and how it may be presented.

- **FDA Issues:** Food, drug, and cosmetic laws vary widely from country to country. You may need to reformulate your product's ingredients. You may find yourself forced to manufacture within the country. Get an early start on labeling since this may slow you down considerably. Get yourself to a lawyer knowledgeable in FDA-type law.

- **Product Compliance:** Check out the government standards for manufacturing with respect to your product. Your product may need to be manufactured within the country. Specific types of products may have their own regulations within the country. You will need to check out your entire product line on this point.

- **Intellectual Property:** In addition to trademarks, you may need to register patents for your products in the country. You may need to check out restrictions regarding transfer of intellectual property, such as software licenses.

- **Immigration:** You will be sending key employees from company headquarters to work for indefinite periods within the country. You need to check out short-term and long-term business visas or other necessary documentation for ongoing residency and local employment.

- **Language:** Verify language restrictions for labeling and literature. In some countries, you may be required to have dual-language labeling.

- **Banking:** There will be large-scale movement of money in and out of countries. You need to verify restrictions on currency movement across borders and whether profits can be repatriated to the home country or must be reinvested in the foreign country.

- **International Sponsoring:** Every company has its own unique method for international sponsoring. Make sure that the new market is receptive to your method of international sponsoring.

Determine the relationship of sponsoring independent representatives in both the home country and foreign country. Will independent representatives need to sign up country by country, or is the company considering a seamless international sponsoring system with inter-company accounting for commission payments?

- **Customs and Tariffs:** Although more free trade is coming about in the world, you need to explore, in detail, customs and tariff issues with respect to your product into the foreign country. In particular, taxing authorities of foreign countries will pay attention to transfer pricing with respect to both customs issues and tax issues.

- **Taxes:** You need a good overview of national, provincial, sales, value added, and other taxes. Your corporate counsel, tax accountants, and foreign counsel need to advise you on the most tax advantageous method of operating, whether as a subsidiary, an affiliate, a branch office, etc.

- **Corporate Form:** Must you have local ownership and have local residence of shareholders and members of your board of directors? Will your independent reps be considered employees? You need to fully understand what your presence will mean in the foreign country.

- **Manufacturing and Supply Agreements:** Must your manufacturing be local? If you are having local manufacturing, make sure that you have adequately secured, under foreign law, your rights and responsibilities with respect to local vendors and suppliers. This may include both production and trade secret formulas and confidential information protection.

- **Marketing Literature:** Everything that is passed out to the consuming public or your independent reps must be brought up to speed, including independent representative agreements, policies and procedures, compliance with door-to-door sales rules, independent representative cancellation rules, buy-back policies, and termination notices.

- **Advertising:** Before you bring your products into the country, are they required to undergo testing to verify claims that you may make about the product or other specific advertising rules that require compliance?

- **Antitrust and Trade Regulations:** You need to check out restrictions on pricing and relationships with suppliers, vendors, independent representatives, competitors, etc. to verify that you are not in violation of local antitrust and trade regulation rules. For instance, you may ask your independent reps to adhere to suggested prices or trade practices imposed by the company.

Competitors

When working at Melaleuca, ServiceQuest founder Terrel Transtrum learned early on that other direct selling companies were not the competition. For Melaleuca, the competition was Procter and Gamble, the personal care and home products giant.

Similarly, there are different types of competitors in direct selling:

- Traditional companies (non-direct selling) that sell the same or similar products and services
- Direct selling companies that sell the same or similar products and services
- Direct selling companies that offer better income opportunities that will draw independent representatives to them

As you become aware of the strengths and weaknesses of your competitors, you will grow strong and confident. If you are keenly focused on your unique differentiators, the primary one being your culture, you will find that the game of growth will be challenging and fun.

As you go through the strategic planning process, don't skip through the SWOT analysis where you will be guided through the exercise of identifying competitors and creating profiles from which you will learn.

Conclusion

Once you have a strategic plan for your business, you will be ready to take your next steps in making your dream a reality. Complete the following checklist in preparation to move forward.

Essential Action Steps for Launching

☐ Validate your product and concept

☐ Identify your core offering and unique value proposition

☐ Clarify your vision, write your story, and express your values

☐ Write your business plan

☐ Develop your growth and financial projections

☐ Declare your personal goals and business goals

☐ Identify and profile your competitors

Chapter 2
Recruit & Retain

One of the first things you will need to do is build your initial field sales force: the early group of independent representatives who will kick-start your business. We constantly hear people say, "I just need to get 1,000 or 1,500 independent reps on board, and then the business will really take off." Well, that's probably true, but you have to take personal responsibility to make it happen. Early efforts will have to be driven by the corporate staff because they will need to find and mentor the first group of field leaders. Those you recruit won't do things they haven't seen you and your team do; you must set the tone.

Along with recruiting comes retention. No matter how good you are at recruiting, unless you can retain your recruits, you will not be able to be as profitable. Like recruiting, you must set the tone for how your company retains your independent reps by putting forth the effort and obtaining the tools needed.

Your Recruiting System

You never get a second chance to make a first impression. People need to be impressed with your company and have a good experience when they join. They must have confidence in you, knowing that those they bring will have a great experience and that you won't embarrass them in any way.

In order to effectively recruit independent reps, your approach must be consistent with your business model and be aligned with what your target reps will find desirable. You should also establish your compensation plan, some early bonuses, and leadership pools that will reward emerging leaders.

There is no magical solution. Building an initial field sales force will require a multifaceted strategy and will take three to six months. Now that we have some basics covered, let's get a bit more specific with ways that you can effectively recruit.

Know Your Target Market

To know your target market, carefully consider the demographics, lifestyle, behavioral patterns, etc. of those you envision using your products and services and joining your sales force. Stay light on your feet because your initial perceptions may not exactly match the reality of those who join.

There are key differences between party plan and network marketing. Party plan company field leaders tend to care less about the compensation plan and more about the product and experiences being offered. Interviews with top field leaders of large party plan companies have shown that many people had no intention of earning an income when they signed up. They just loved the product and wanted to get it at the best price, and the way to do that was to become an independent representative for the company. Then at some point in time, the light went on for them, and they said, "Hey, people are making money doing this. I probably can too."

On the other hand, network marketing leaders will be attracted to join because of the income opportunity. Product quality is important, but it must produce a powerful income opportunity.

Overall, both party plan and network marketing reps are attracted by a cause that will help make the world a better place. They want a unique story to tell and that story must revolve around the product and serves being offered, the company and key leaders involved, and the income opportunity.

Use Your Resources

There are several different kinds of helpful resources that you may have available to you. If you have an existing product line being sold and marketed through other channels, think about how you can leverage that side of your business and its customer base to find leaders.

Another way is to let your corporate staff know that as you prepare to launch they need to start talking to friends and family because some of your initial leaders can be found among their acquaintances. If there are people with direct selling experience who have shown interest in your progress, keep them informed and meet with them about early recruiting strategies.

For party plan companies, one of the best ways to recruit independent reps is at parties. Leverage all your home-office team's personal contacts to identify hosts and hold test parties as early as possible. Build excitement at these parties, and let the attendees know that you're looking for leaders to drive your company and that they'll be generously rewarded through your compensation plan and founder's group program.

Use Public Relations

Work with the media to get coverage of the launch of your business. It's often free and will lend credibility to your business because it is perceived as "unbiased coverage" of what you are doing. You can attract support and coverage by focusing on your unique product or the launch of a new local business. Center the coverage on meetings, events, tours of the home office, product demonstrations, etc. This will drive you to places where you can meet people, build relationships, tell your story, capture names, and follow up. Use these opportunities to promote your website. Remember to capture leads and follow up on them.

Use Events

We cannot overstate the power of early events, such as appropriate trade shows, county fairs, and community events that you create. These events provide an opportunity for you to tell your story, show your products, meet prospects, build relationships, and allow prospects to meet one another and develop a sense of belonging within your young field team.

Start with Your Home Town

Always start in your hometown or city and other communities within easy driving range. Focus on the areas where you have friends or family members who will assist in your recruiting activities or where there are potential independent reps. This will keep costs down and allow you to have people come to your home office and meet with corporate leaders. It will also make it easier to stage recruiting events. In addition, advertising costs can be very reasonable in smaller regional newspapers, regional television and radio stations, and even billboards. You can literally saturate your region and gain strong momentum.

This worked for Melaleuca, a $700 million company in our hometown of Idaho Falls, Idaho. At the base of the Teton Mountain Range, about an hour's drive from Idaho Falls, is the small community of Driggs, Idaho. With a population of 2,583 people, Driggs is home to several of the millionaire earners at Melaleuca; these are the locals that gave Melaleuca a chance when it was starting and took it to the nation through their friends and family.

Use Key People

Take advantage of founders or people who are central to the product story. Use these people effectively in public relations activities, at events, on conference calls, on your website, etc. People want to be led. Early field leaders value a strong personal connection to key people in your company.

Use the Internet

Make sure you have a top-notch website, and work with technology specialists to drive traffic to that site, or to a splash page if your website isn't available yet. To be effective in internet marketing, employ the services of a marketing firm that specializes in internet marketing. Their efforts will generally focus on two areas: search engine optimization and social media marketing. In short, your goal is to "create a buzz" about what you're doing.

Be sure to capture the contact information of those who visit your website or splash page and have a designated team member call them, build a personal relationship with them, and, if possible, bring them into a three-way call with one of your early field leaders. Offer a pre-launch newsletter so you can use to keep in touch with prospects and keep them informed of your progress.

Build Excitement

As you begin to attract some early leaders, pour gas on their fire of excitement while it's burning hot. Don't let it cool off. Turn your corporate office into an exciting recruiting center. Provide cubicles and phones. Allow emerging leaders to work together to compile their contact lists and share approaches that work well.

Provide events and conference calls they can invite prospects to attend. Have key corporate leaders get on three-way calls with them. Keep a scoreboard in the home office. Have competitions. Offer cash incentives. Have conference calls with emerging leaders outside your area to share ideas. Get people excited. Consider bringing in promising leaders for a week or two to create "sales teams" that make prospect lists, initiate contacts from the office, and derive energy and support at this critical point for your company.

Follow Pockets of Energy

As leaders begin to emerge in other geographic areas, you'll start to see pockets of energy arise as people become are excited and work hard at building the business. Support these people with corporate-sponsored events in their areas. Give them what they need to succeed.

Recruit to Retain

You want people who are a good fit for the long haul. A couple of key principles to follow and to teach your emerging leaders are 1) don't oversell, 2) manage each new recruit's expectations, and 3) provide exceptional support to new recruits. Make sure they have a clear picture of the benefits of being involved and what they'll have to do to experience those benefits.

Use Prelaunch Enrollment

To further fuel excitement for growth and enrollments, many companies encourage prelaunch enrolling to secure their position in the organization. Then, when you're ready to "go live," you can process payments and enrollments by entering the data into your system. As a rule of thumb, don't do this until about two months before your "go live" date.

Use Advertising Judiciously

There are a few reputable network marketing and direct sales publications that focus on independent representatives as their readers. Consider advertising with these publications but be aware of costs and response rates. Getting involved with leading publications early on can increase your company's visibility and advertising at select websites.

Leading publications include:

- Direct Selling News: www.directsellingnews.com
- Direct Selling Women's Alliance (DSWA): www.mydswa.org
- Direct Selling Association (DSA): www.dsa.org

Be aware that widespread advertising campaigns can be very costly and are generally more effective for network marketing recruiting than for party plan companies. As mentioned earlier, focused advertising campaigns in small markets can be more affordable and effective and can be used to drive traffic to meetings or events that you host. When prospects in a community see an article about your company in the paper, hear about it on the radio, see an advertisement on cable TV, or see it on a billboard, they conclude that "there must be something to this," and they often don't consider that the coverage might be only local.

Do an internet search for "work-at-home moms," "network marketing opportunities," "party plan opportunities," and other terms that relate to your product or service to identify websites you could advertise on.

Focus on Specific Market Segments

There may be specific market segments that will be strongly and naturally attracted to your product and business opportunity. Think about the different markets that would best fit your product whether it is chiropractors, students, fitness trainers, health stores, or craft stores. Once you have an idea specific market segments that you can approach, find ways to advertise to those specific markets.

Independent Rep Retention Strategies

The fact is that 80 percent of attrition in the first year is the average for network marketing companies and 60 percent is the average for party plan companies.[4] This means that if 100 people join your network marketing company in January, twenty of them will still be active in December. If you do nothing proactive to increase your retention you will perform at that level, and it will have a devastating impact on your ability to be profitable. There is good news though. You can beat the average and have a profitable, healthy, long-term business if you focus not only on recruiting, but also on retaining.

---

4   Four separate studies concluded this, run by ServiceQuest®, the DSA, Harvard Business Review, and Wirthlin.

We have studied the principles of companies that have the highest retention rates, and we have incorporated that knowledge into our philosophies and systems. We present many of those key principles and specifics in duplicable practices so that you can learn from them.

There are three reasons we believe increasing retention is so vital to your business:

- You receive a return on your investment. A study published by the Boston-based firm of Bain and Company concludes that a five percent improvement in retention can result in as much as 25 to 100 percent increase in profits. Moreover, a mere two percent improvement in retention is the equivalent of a 10 percent decrease in expenses.

- The cost of finding a new customer is four to six times the cost of retaining an existing customer, and the cost of finding a new independent representative is six to eight times the cost of retaining an existing rep.

- Retention is the number-one cure for momentum blues because it is a morale and momentum driver. Consistently high retention levels boost morale. People feel they're part of a winning team as they see others stay involved and succeed.

The Retention Myth

There is a myth that prevails in the industry: "You can't measure retention and you can't impact retention, so just out-enroll attrition." We believe that this retention myth is false. Not only can you measure and impact retention, your retention levels actually drive your recruiting requirements, growth, and profitability.

For example, suppose your goal is 1,000 active reps in your business. Your company's annual retention rate is 20 percent (the norm for network marketing companies). You will need 5,000 recruits to meet the goal of 1,000 active. Now here's the point, by increasing your retention rate by five percent you will need only 4,000 recruits, instead of 5,000 to meet your goal of 1,000 active. That's 20 percent fewer recruits needed to meet your goal. That's the power of leveraging retention.

Where Does Retention Happen?

As independent reps become associated with your business, they enter an activity lifecycle. Picture a timeline moving from left to right. The timeline begins with pre-enrollment, then it moves to sign-up through the first 13 weeks. Next it goes into full activity (this step varies in length depending on the person), and finally, it ends with inactivity. At each phase, the level of activity (usually measured by purchases and enrollments) is different. The activity level usually follows a bell-shaped curve, with the highest levels of activity being over the center of the full activity phase and the lowest levels being just before inactivity.

Retention consists of lengthening the period of activity and increasing the level of activity. Retention activities tend to happen between the corporate office, the independent representatives, and the customers as well as between only independent representatives and customers. In other words, we have corporate-to-field retention activities and field-to-field retention activities.

Becoming Good at Retention

The basic principles of retention have been around for centuries. Retention-based management is our standardization of a phenomenon we've observed and analyzed over the course of our work studying the problems and successes of more than a hundred companies.

What sets the best companies apart from the others is a measurable advantage in the retention of independent representatives, customers, and employees. We found that when a company had unusually high retention, it was also delivering superior value to the field and employees while generating inexplicably strong cash flows to fund growth.

To maximize your ability to have good retention you must:

- **Take Responsibility:** Retention is too important to delegate. The responsibility for field retention belongs squarely on the CEO's desk, where it can get the same kind of attention that is lavished on issues like cash flow, profits, and FDA.

  To make retention work, most established businesses must make fundamental changes in their business practices and policy administration. The longer you take to change and adopt best-in-class retention practices, the higher the cost of that change. So regardless of where you are in your business maturity or growth cycle, start the retention process now.

- **Engage Retention Champions:** Find leaders in your company that will help you to champion retention, work its details, and become an expert of retention initiatives.

- **Create Your Retention Dashboard:** You must be able to measure, and even predict, where you're going in terms of retention. You must determine whether your changes in practices are having an impact. To do so establish a retention dashboard that will show the key retention indicators.

- **Implement Consistent, Repeatable Retention Practices:** Know what these best-in-class practices are and integrate them into your business at all levels.

- **Keep Measuring, Monitoring, and Improving:** Continuously monitoring your retention dashboard will allow you to track key retention indicators and gauge progress and return on investment as you improve your processes and practices.

When we begin assisting our clients in evaluating their retention health, we start with four key questions:

- How well do you understand retention?
- Do you measure retention?
- Do your systems support retention?
- Does your team (both corporate and field) possess the knowledge, skills, and motivation to support and implement retention initiatives?

Retention Processes

At a very basic level, your company must have some key operating processes in place in order to move forward with more advanced retention principles and practices. The six basic processes are enrollment processing, order processing, payment processing, returns and exchanges, commission processing, and customer service administration. If you feel you need a tune up in any of these areas, your ServiceQuest coach will work with you to help you get up to speed.

Retention Principles

Listed below are principles of retention that set the stage for your advanced work in the dozens of retention best practices that you will master as you launch your company:

- **Value:** Creating value for customers and independent representatives is the foundation of any successful business system. Value produces loyalty, and loyalty in turn drives retention and builds growth, profit, and additional value. Value must be created and adequately conveyed at all levels of the corporation and in the field. Make sure that your value elements are organized and presented in a way that consistently conveys them to the world and that the features and benefits of those unique value elements are clearly identified and trained on so that sales, upsells, and service efforts are enhanced. You must methodically build this practice into your infrastructure, and over time you'll experience the rewards of your preparation.

- **Know, Manage, and Exceed Expectations:** From the very beginning of the life cycle of a customer or independent representative, you must know their expectations, do all you can to manage those expectations, and deploy all your resources to exceed their expectations. Independent reps come with a high degree of energy and drive when they first join you. Put into place the methods for assuring that they experience immediate success that meet their expectations and help to fund their progress. Also, make sure that the enrollment process includes clearly defined steps for discovering the expectations of new independent reps and that you're enthusiastically greeting new customers and independent reps as they enroll with your company.

- **Service:** Service begins with a true desire to enhance the customer experience. It extends to the people that you bring into the organization (both inside as well as in the field), and it incorporates systems and processes, not just smiles. Retention leaders provide the training and support for their front-line employees to find a way to say "yes" to requests. This can be a daunting practice to implement unless you have some key elements in place: system for contact tracking, clear parameters for employees to work within, skills for making judgment calls, accountability for decisions rendered, and money spent to build goodwill. These are all attainable with careful planning and implementation. The benefits can be enormous as the company gains consistency while it earns the highest marks in service.

- **Leadership:** Shape the vision, provide the passion, and lead the way. Every corporate staff member must lead by example. In the field, identify leaders, build leaders, and make them successful. The organization structure, when designed a certain way, can make the difference between a half billion-dollar company with an astounding service reputation and a struggling enterprise that is trying to figure itself out. It can be as simple as removing the barriers and restrictions that prevent a customer service manager from reporting directly to the CEO.

A Successful Founder's Group Program

Are any of these questions on your mind?

- How do I respond when I get approached by an independent representative who is a "big hitter" (self-proclaimed or legitimate) and says, "I can bring to your company an entire organization of 1,000 people with me"? What are you going to do for me?"
- How do I attract "big hitters"? What are they looking for?
- How do I promote early, strong, sustainable growth in my independent representative base?

These are common questions that are answered, at least in part, by developing and implementing an effective Founder's Group Program. Here are a few basic points about this kind of program:

- A Founder's Group Program is a one-time opportunity that comes along early in the life of a start-up. It is meant to reward those early entrepreneurial independent reps who take a chance on your start-up company and who undertake the hard work of building the initial independent representative base.
- A Founder's Group Program has to be positioned as a race against time for it to be effective. There needs to be a deadline.
- Becoming a Founding Independent Representative needs to be earned, and, once earned, it's a title that is not easily lost. Now,

they may not always be paid as a founding independent rep, but they will not likely lose the title or the special seat at the annual convention.

- Ongoing financial rewards are earned. Founding Independent Representatives have to keep working and building for it to mean anything to them financially.

- Your compensation plan designer should build the Founder's Group Program into your compensation plan. This will ensure that the rewards are in harmony with your overall compensation plan and that you can afford the payout.

A Word of Advice

Don't make special deals with independent representatives! Don't pay them retainers! Don't offer them a single and only front-line position under which the entire field organization is built! Don't!

Why? Well, first of all, the best reps won't require a special offer. As long as you have a great product and an effective compensation program, that's all you need to attract them. Second, the reps who typically ask for those types of deals will usually stay with you for a short period of time and then move on, asking for (and often getting) a special deal from another start-up company.

Communicate Clearly

Now a couple of key points regarding communication. A Founder's Group Program is available to all independent representatives, not just your favorite reps or those who have the look and feel of a big hitter. You'll be surprised at which reps will wind up being the top sellers. Because of this, communicate the Founder's Group Program clearly to all new independent representatives until the deadline is past.

Also, be sure to watch your database reports and pay attention to those who are progressing towards becoming a Founding Independent Representative. Call them. Encourage them. See what you can do to help them make it. See what barriers you can remove.

Founder's Group Program Bonus

While there are many ways to design a Founder's Group Program, here's one way we've found to be effective.

First, choose a rank from your compensation plan that must be achieved by a specific deadline. For example, let's say you launch your company in January, and the requirement for your founder's group is that all those who achieve the rank of Platinum Independent Representative by January of the following year earn the title of Founding Independent Representative.

The rank and deadline you choose are some of your most important decisions you will make in designing this program. If you make it too easy, it won't mean anything, and you'll have too many founding independent representatives. If you make it too hard, no one will believe they can do it, and it won't have its intended motivating impact. Counsel with your compensation plan designer to decide what works best. In addition, tying the Founding Independent Representative rank directly to the compensation plan keeps reps focused on earning their income based on making the most of your compensation plan.

Second, define the rules of participation clearly in the compensation plan, and be sure to educate all new independent representatives on the rules of participation. Specify how they will be paid. Let them know they have to be active in the rank you've specified in order to be paid the Founder's Group Bonus. If they are not active, they may not lose the title of Founding Independent Representative, but they won't be paid according to the rules of the Founder's Group Bonus.

Some companies don't give independent rep the Founder's Group Bonus until they reach a certain level of gross sales. This protects the early cash flow and break-even profitability of the company. Other companies choose to limit the bonus pool to a certain percentage of gross sales.

Others choose to remove the title of Founding Independent Representative if independent representatives are not active in the specified rank for a certain period of time. Define the rules of the game carefully and clearly. However, having too many rules will make independent representatives lose interest.

Example: Founder's Group Program

To help you understand how the bonus program might work, we have provided a detailed example. See the Figure 2–1 to see an illustration of this example.

Let's say the Founder's Group Bonus Pool is a monthly pool that is a percentage of any new "high mark" in monthly company gross sales. If the highest sales volume in any given previous month is $50,000, and the current month sales are $100,000, then we have a new "high mark," and the difference between the two is $50,000. Let's say the Founder's Group Bonus Pool is 10% of the "high mark," so in this case, it would be $5,000.

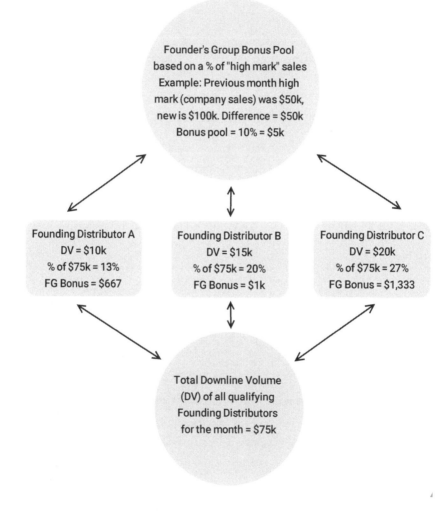

Figure 2-1: Founder's Group Bonus Example

Recognition

While it is easy to focus on the bonus numbers, don't overlook the power of recognition. The title of Founding Independent Representative is coveted! Having your name splashed on the company newsletter, being walked across the stage at the first annual convention, sitting at a special table at the formal convention dinner—those things are all huge! People love to be recognized. So, capitalize on it.

The Role of CEO in Sales and Recruiting

Direct selling CEOs are under tremendous pressure. We maintain that direct selling is quite possibly the most stressful business model because it combines all the moving parts of traditional business with the weird and whacky (there's no other way to describe it) world of a strictly volunteer sales force.

The pressures of operations and administration are enough to keep a CEO in his or her office around the clock. Yet, the most important proclamation we can make about the role of the CEO in sales and recruiting is that sales and recruiting is the main job. Whenever direct selling companies experience decline in sales and recruiting, CEOs either cower or they go out and work directly with their people. Those who cower don't last long, and neither do their companies. Those who get to work with their people turn the tides of momentum and make growth happen.

In the most dramatic of economic times, whether in the recessionary years of the 1980s or in the more recent heavy recession, it's not surprising that some direct selling companies close down and others break records. CEOs that close down their companies have at least one of two things in common:

- They give in to the notions that people are not spending money, they're not working their businesses, and times are hard
- They do not have products and services that deliver genuine value

On the other hand, those that have companies that soar in both good times and hard times have several things in common:

- Their corporate leaders are legitimately optimistic and realistic
- They are accessible, available, and found among the foot soldiers
- They communicate
- They're transparent and forthright
- They encourage dreaming and devote themselves to helping those dreams to come true
- They maintain consistency in product quality, commissions, and service
- They innovate
- They put the interests and success of their independent reps first and foremost while maintaining appropriate corporate controls and fiscal responsibility

CEOs and corporate executives don't get lost in their own importance. They know their roles are deeply grounded in selling and recruiting as they build companies that transport dreams into realities. In the end, it's about the culture they create.

Communication

Direct selling is all about relationships, and the core of any relationship is communication. The company has been described as the "nerve center" of the field's business operation, and, to the field, the company has primary accountability for most communications.

Research shows the number one reason independent representatives leave an organization is poor communication. Those who use ineffective communications can include sponsors who don't support and communicate adequately with those they bring in, subpar customer service managers and organizations within the company, company leadership (including marketing and sales teams at corporate), and upline leaders who do not train the people in their organization. Without effective communication, nobody wins. Your best chance at winning is by taking initiative to design and champion an effective company-wide communications strategy.

Communications in the direct selling environment occur in three groupings: company-to-company, company-to-field, and field-to-field. Each communications grouping has its own requirements, and an effective over-all communications system takes all three groupings into account.

Effective communication is about achieving dialogue, maintaining respect, and sharing a clearly defined purpose. Dialogue is the free flow of meaning between two parties.[5] Whether we are talking about internal communications at a corporate level between individuals or departments, communications between the customer service organization and the field, or communications between and among independent representatives—the goal is the same: to achieve dialogue. Respect and mutual purpose help to keep everybody in dialogue, resulting in growth and progress.

Creating an Effective Communications Plan

At its basic level, an effective communication plan is designed with the Four C's at its foundation:

- **Calendar:** This considers the schedules for when communications go out. We have learned that the predictable cycles are still the most effective, whether it's a weekly president's message, a month-ly newsletter, an email series, or a special "Breaking News" that is only used when something is truly newsworthy.

- **Content:** With increasingly sophisticated independent represen-tatives and customers, no one likes to feel that he or she is being forced into a one-size-fits-all communication. Each will pick and choose what they're interested in, so be sure that the content matches the intended audience and that the content is consistent. Also, make sure that the selected calendar and channel(s) will sup-port your communications objectives.

- **Channels:** Go where the people are, meet them on their terms, and reach them in the ways they like to be reached. This requires that you have a basic understanding of your company's demo-graphics. Univera, for example, offers a product line that is popular among an aging demographic, so they are not as "Twitter-prone" as the edgy reps at AGEL who stay on the cutting edge of "cool." Neither is right or wrong, both seem to understand how to use the many media channels available to them.

---

5   Crucial Conversations: Tools for Talking When Stakes are High.

- **Constituents:** These are the recipients of your communications, which are not only demographics of age, region, etc., but also the profiles of their interests. Remember that the motivation for each person to join is different. In other words, someone who joins the company to try out your product may evolve in interest levels and might even become your next superstar builder. Keep this in mind as you create your communications plan.

Direct Selling Communications Strategy

In addition to the basic "Four C's" presented above, the most effective direct selling communications systems have eight pillars: welcome system, training center, direct coaching, newsletters and emails, conference calls, support services, recognition, and advisory councils.

Figure 2–2: The 8 Pillars of Effective Direct Selling Communications Systems

Pillar 1: Welcome System

The welcome system is the pivotal communication point for all new customers and independent representatives that join your company. The goal is to establish credibility, help build belief, and manage expectations while fueling hope and creating an environment that nurtures success.

Highly effective elements include:

- Starter Kit with welcome letter and clearly defined next steps
- Auto-response emails that engage and motivate
- Outbound welcome contacts from customer service staff
- Video welcomes
- Package inserts
- Orientation at your company's training center

Effective messages and templates include:

- Auto-response that the company has received the new application
- Separate email welcoming the new recruit
- Postcard/letter/email with information designed to ensure a successful start-up
- Emails notifying when the starter kit and first order have shipped
- Communication designed to channel energies toward training
- Congratulations on "Certification" training
- Weekly email offering words of wisdom and support

As your abilities and resources expand, keep an eye on what gets added. Be consistent and focus on creating an extraordinary experience through caring and thoughtful contacts along the way.

Pillar 2: Training Center

People learn in different ways. Some learn through reading while others learn by observing, and some prefer to learn through listening while others learn through hands-on training. Many do well in an environment that combines two or more of these methods.

We believe in the power of an effective training center; thus, we have designed our entire white-label and custom client training for delivery through the ServiceQuest® Training Center. This is a platform that becomes your company's training platform, starting with the option to use it as one of your company's unique differentiators.

Through your training system, you will want to cover the basics such as policies and procedures, compensation plan, products, recruiting, selling, and business planning.

In addition to an effective web-based training center, other communications tools include the training manual in the starter kit, online PowerPoint with audio (delivered through the training center), online certification, and one-to-one field coaching.

Pillar 3: Direct Coaching

The best coaching happens live, whether in person or via electronic means such as live GoToMeeting® webinars and live broadcasts. Leaders of great companies are always on the road to visit and work with members in the sales force.

Over the years, we've observed that when there is a downturn in recruiting and sales, the CEO needs to respond by visiting the sales force. Not surprisingly, when they do this, recruiting and sales begin to grow again. This is the essence of effective selling and coaching.

One-on-one contact with independent reps at their locations, when economically feasible, builds strong pockets of belief, energy, and growth. Carefully planned coaching meetings will always get results. Whether you join existing meetings and events and/or hold special company events, payback is often immediate.

Pillar 4: Newsletters and Emails

Newsletters are important. When distributed via email, you can track data that otherwise is unknown with printed newsletters. A monthly newsletter is the norm. Look carefully into newsletter services that specialize in direct selling such as IMN (I Make News: www.imninc.com), which is credited for its role in contributing to an amazing growth surge for Scentsy starting around 2009.

Emails are important, but keep in mind that an email is not communication. Email is a medium or channel through which you can send information that reaches a diminishing percentage of people. Your best outcomes happen when emails are consistent, targeted, predictable in content and timing, and useful.

Topics that help independent reps to feel emotionally connected with the company, whether shared via newsletters or emails, include:

- Product launches, updates, enhancements
- Product news, testimonials, and information
- New or changes to policies and procedures
- Company milestones and insider news
- Upcoming events
- Success stories
- Top performing reps and their secrets
- Contest scoreboards and winners
- Educational tools
- Practical tips and useful information on any aspect of the customer or rep experience
- Congratulations and welcomes (new staff, new independent representatives)
- Recognition and rank advancements

Pillar 5: Conference Calls

Team conference calls work for many. One of the premier field leaders we've had the privilege of associating with reminded us that every Monday morning she has a quick conference call with her fourteen personal recruits to provide vision and leadership, check in with them, help them get focused on their goals as they make their work plan.

Topics for conference calls should be selected to meet the needs of those who attend (or should be attending). Conference calls commonly include one or more of the following:

- Training
- Policy and procedure updates
- Sales tools
- Recognition
- Promotions
- Contest winners

- Q & A
- Team building

Pillar 6: Support Services

We are particularly fond of the customer service reps that don their headsets and turn calls and contacts into minute-by-minute successes. The interaction (such as short hold times, scripted verbal insertions, and call closes) gives rise to potentially the greatest communications opportunities that the company has available. The key is to carefully and purposefully construct the experience.

Questions and areas to prepare for are covered separately in the section for staff selection and development. For this section, these are high-level areas to consider:

- Compensation questions in all their varieties
- Qualification and rank advancement questions
- Special orders and topics related to the order system
- Policies and procedures and what they mean; how to apply them
- Technical questions for use of web, technology, and other tools
- Customer orders, returns, exchanges, and refunds
- Becoming an independent representative; locating a sponsor
- Company information, including who we are
- How to keep the company legal and on track
- How to get a suggestion to someone who cares

Pillar 7: Recognition

Direct selling is a relationship business. At the heart of relationships are gratitude, honor, and respect. These are shown in many ways, but the essence is recognition. The results are worth every effort and dime, measured in loyalty, retention, and lasting profits.

Direct selling reps are not employees who report to work daily. They are volunteer workers—independent contractors who operate their own businesses. What they do is up to them. The company presents the path and structure, products, and encouragement.

In preparing for launch, plan to recognize your independent reps early and often. This comes in the form of notes, calls, and in-person praising at live events and local meetings. A good compensation plan will reward certain behaviors—selling, recruiting, managing, leading, and retaining. Recognition will reinforce the behaviors and draw attention to success factors that transcend the compensation plan.

A common budget range for awards, incentives, and recognition runs from two percent to five percent with three percent being the most common budget. Of course, new companies typically don't have budgets for leadership cruises and trips. Yet, meaningful recognition can be as simple as exclusive logo merchandise (not otherwise available for purchase). We recommend that our clients "borrow" from the breakage of a new compensation plan to help fund recognition until sales volume sustains the intended budget. Build into the annual conference plan all things recognition, such as giving recognized independent reps different color nametags or lanyards, special pins, special seating at the event, and invitations to special luncheons.

Keep in mind that people respond to recognition in a variety of ways, yet there are common elements of successful incentives and recognition. Be sure to recognize not only top achievers but also all who achieve targets you've set.

Pillar 8: Advisory Councils

One of the most powerful communications tools available to companies is the field advisory council. Such a council is comprised of field leaders who meet with the corporate team in a spirit of collaboration. Variations in councils, member selection criteria, venues, purposes, outputs, and frequency present an interesting challenge. One thing is for sure, field advisory councils work, and great field advisory councils work great!

As you gain early independent representatives, take note of the reps that you feel have the greatest leadership potential. You can invite six to eight of these individuals to serve as your Interim Field Advisory Council." They'll have the opportunity to review key elements of your business (such as your compensation plan) as those elements are developed. This will do two things: 1) get them bought in, energized, and committed as leaders and 2) provide you with important feedback.

When you launch, you will announce the criteria (metrics such as number of parties, recruits, and personal and group sales) for selecting your first Field Advisory Council, which should be selected six months after launch. In effect, you say, "Here's how we're going to keep score. Here are the ground rules for getting into the inner circle." The Interim Advisory Council will serve as your council until that time.

Here we present the key considerations for selecting a council, assembling the council, and getting full mutual benefit from council involvement in the strategic planning and tactical implementation of your company's growth and retention plan. In presenting our ideas and observations, we presume that the reader has at least a basic understanding of the dynamics and politics of selection and management of field councils. We also assume that the reader is proficient in the many facets of meeting planning, along with the logistics of venue selection, transportation, physical facilities, and accommodations required to make an on-site field council a successful event.

The four areas we present to help you in assembling your council are purpose, criteria and selection, agenda, and helpful tips:

- **Purpose:** The purposes for which a field advisory council may be established are numerous. They may be a one-time council to solve a significant problem. They may be convened for a period, such as six months or a year, in order to oversee or participate in an important project. They may even be a rotating council with evolving duties and areas of focus. Regardless of the purpose for establishing a council, the effective field advisory councils have several very important things in common.

  ☐ Councils provide power. It is important to be strategic in who you place in your council and who you leave in the field. Put people in the area where they will be of most use to your company because convening a council can take your best workers out of the field which may cause a loss of leadership within the field.

  ☐ Councils can represent the voice of the field and then carry the message of the company back to the field. The most effective councils are comprised of leaders who are involved in the field. They are constantly testing the pulse, handling objections, making presentations, and enrolling new recruits. Their top priority is with their people, and the good ones know what's going on within the company. Involvement in any council is secondary in overall importance.

☐ Councils provide a potentially effective group for test markets, focus groups, and advisory services. We say "potentially" because, again, if the right people make it to the council and if you really listen to what they have to say and then act on it, you will enjoy stronger growth and retention.

Some of the purposes for which councils are assembled and convened include the following:

☐ Periodic (quarterly/monthly) communications between corporate and field leaders

☐ Frequent "download" of important lessons learned in the field, noting what's working and what's not working

☐ Regular off-loading of concerns, objections, and complaints that commonly land with the field leaders but don't always seem to be heard at the corporate office

☐ Confidential testing of concepts, upgrades and improvements of products, compensation, service, etc.

☐ Brainstorming solutions to extremes (downturns or fast growth)

☐ Recognition, bonding and team building, instruction, training and development

- **Criteria and Selection:** Bear in mind that the relationship aspect of direct selling (the true power of network marketing) is found in the interpersonal skills and persuasive abilities of the sales leaders. Thus, if the selection is left for political positioning when criteria are too subjective, the credibility and effectiveness of the council will be dead in the water.

The only thing that endures through the years is the establishment of clear, objective selection criteria. Much like an Olympic event, those who are sent to represent their countries are selected based solely on their performances. Thus, we strongly advocate the establishment and consistent administration of criteria that are visible, measurable, and attainable.

The criteria are closely tied to the purpose of the council. For instance, if the purpose of the council is to advise the company on new aspects, enhancements, or changes in the company's compensation plan, the criteria might include:

☐ Leaders with fast-growth experience in the past twelve months (new enrollments, overall sales, etc.)

☐ Leaders with organizations that have demonstrated the highest percentage of new recruits that select auto ship when they join

☐ Leaders with the highest percentage of downline organizations that participate in company training programs, attend regional meetings, etc.

For a list of councils, the purpose/role of each one, and the potential criteria to use for selecting members, visit Table 2–1 of the Appendix.

- **Agenda:** Each agenda will be different, depending upon the objectives for convening a council. We offer an agenda as representative of the most important field council meetings. Visit Table 2–2 in the Appendix for a samples of an executive leadership council agenda.

Many variations on the agenda will be appropriate. Just remember that one of the most important considerations for any field council meeting is the facilitation of communication, idea sharing, strengthening relationships, and building trust.

- **Helpful Tips:** Listed below are a variety of suggestions and tips garnered from years of experience.

☐ Establish a charter that will guide the council and follow the charter. For an example of a field advisory council charter, see Table 2–3 in the Appendix.

☐ Weeks before a scheduled council meeting contact each participant and invite them to fax or email their major concerns, problems in the field, attitudes about the company, areas requiring attention, and/or improvements. This will permit your management team to understand the concerns in the field, address them ahead of arrival, and plan a discussion for the council meeting.

☐ Discuss the field concerns with individual leaders ahead of the council meeting. At the beginning of the meeting, address the common/universal issues. Get them completely aired and addressed so that the remaining time can be used productively.

☐ Prepare meaningful recognition for council members. As they participate in the inner circle, the recognition that they receive will often represent the high point of their careers.

☐ Begin each meeting with a review of the ground rules or meeting guidelines and interpersonal rules that encourage high levels of candor and productivity for the safety created for participants.

☐ Always apply the protocol of effective meetings, including room layout, scribe, creature comforts, and professional courtesies that make the meeting a memorable experience.

Conclusion

• We believe recruiting and retention go hand in hand. You must personally see to establishing effective systems for both recruiting and retaining. When these are established, your company can flourish through maintaining profitable independent reps. Below are the key action steps to take to create your recruiting and retention systems.

Essential Action Steps for Launching

☐ Define your awards, incentives, and recognition programs

☐ Create your retention plan and

☐ Create your plan for recruiting the first 500 reps

☐ Plan promotions and contests

☐ Design tools and materials

☐ Create product packs and rep kits

☐ Create your founder's organization plan and

☐ Design your communication plan

Chapter 3
Sales

The main sales force for a direct selling company is made up of "volunteer" independent representatives. Because it is likely that your sales force will be inexperienced in sales, you will have to provide them with every possible tool to help them succeed and, in turn, help your company succeed.

The Success Cycle

All successful direct selling companies realize that the majority of people who join their companies and seek an income opportunity are not, nor do they wish to be, professional sales people. In fact, the thought of outright selling typically scares them to death. They don't know what to say or when to say it. And they don't know what to do to build their business. So, you have to give them a simple, proven step by step system to follow, something they can do over and over again. And the more times they repeat it the more success they will experience in building their business and their income. This system is called the *success cycle*.

Generic Principles

Great success cycles are built on four distinct phases, which are repeated in a continuous cycle (see Figure 3–1).

The first phase, Assess and Set Goals, requires self-assessment and setting goals to improve. This is something that new recruits must be directed to do and that experienced independent reps must be reminded to do. This phase helps everyone stay focused on what is important.

Once you have a goal, the second phase, Create an Action Plan, can start. This is where your goals are turned into a plan. The third phase, Implement Your Plan, closely follows as that plan starts to come into play. The second and third steps require careful mentoring and support early in the rep's experience with the company for it to become a habit.

The fourth phase, Report and Celebrate, cannot be overlooked. Reporting and celebrating helps to improve motivation and assure that the cycle will be repeated.

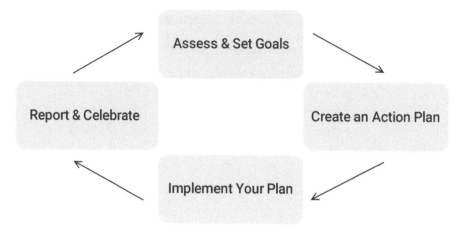

Figure 3–1: The Success Cycle.

A complete cycle can take as little as a few hours or a day, and your company's training systems—from day one after enrollment—should be designed to train, encourage, and reinforce the supporting behaviors.

Fast Start Success Elements

The success cycle begins for all new independent reps with a fast start based on six foundational elements. Think of these elements as your key opportunities to provide the training, tools, and motivation necessary to enable the new rep to launch the success cycle into motion:

- **The First Order:** Having new recruits place their first order early will expose them to the order process, company systems and personnel, and products at the most advantageous time. Done right, the process should be easily duplicated so that recruit can see a clear path to fulfilling their own goals. It is also the gateway for many recruiters to earn special incentives on orders placed by new recruits. Value packs and special promotions can provide an exciting experience for new recruits, offer opportunities to boost earnings for the recruiters, and increase volumes for upline commissions.

- **The TLC Contact:** Studies show that on average, it takes eight negative experiences to overcome a positive bond that a customer or business builder has with a company—if that bond is forged ahead of the negative experiences. This powerful knowledge indicates that the proper TLC (tender loving care) contacts at the earliest possible stages of the relationship will forge the bonds that can withstand eroding influences, giving your new recruit their best chances of long-term success with their clients and with working with your business.

  - ☐ The most effective TLC contacts occur within the first 72 hours of sign-up. Effective points of contact include telephone calls from upline and/or corporate, email, direct mail, postcards, inserts in orders, and independent surveys and welcome calls. These efforts should be carefully orchestrated through a well-defined system so that everybody knows their role and can work together.

- **The Support Team:** The support team consists of the sponsor, upline leaders, corporate support centers, and the company website. By making sure new recruits know where to get the support they need, their foundation grows stronger. Surveys with top business builders from a variety of companies around the nation reveal that personal mentoring and handholding during the fast-start period forges enduring, profitable business relationships. They unanimously agree that by assisting with contact lists, telephone calls, appointments, presentations, and sign-ups in the early stages helps new recruits discover what works for them while letting the leader oversee and mentor the growth in their organization.

- **Getting Connected:** Getting connected encompasses product experience and knowledge, business plan training, and steps required to get the new recruit solidly connected to the company. This element incorporates training meetings and calls, calendars, emails, company orientations, product introductions, business system introductions, and tools.

- **The Stories:** Each new recruit needs to know and be able to briefly and concisely relate three very important stories: the company story, the product story, and the business story. These can be as simple as a two- or three-sentence explanation that gives new recruits something to say when they have to explain their decision to join the company to family and friends.

- **Goals and Action Plan:** A dream written down becomes a goal. A goal broken down becomes a plan. A plan converted to action makes the dream come true. The major goals are income goals, rank/status goals, and other relevant personal goals. The key here is that this foundational element must be built into the fast-start phase and give guidance in setting meaningful and attainable goals, managing expectations, and creating a daily work plan that will lead to near-term successes. Near-term successes fuel the big goals that can fulfill dreams. Make sure that early money is available and meaningful.

Revisiting and Refining After Launch

As you launch your company, you will devise your initial success cycle—perhaps with the help of a few of your first field leaders. As the months unfold, leaders will emerge in your field organization. These will be people who are not only effective at building their sales and their team but at retaining those they recruit. They will adapt your success cycle to their style and approach. Pay attention to what they're doing, and don't be afraid to adapt the company-sponsored success cycle to replicate and reinforce they're effective methods. This can be a great task for an advisory council.

Building Your Sales Team

The "internal" sales team (the director of sales, vice president of sales, etc.) devote themselves to the success of the field organization. They serve as the company executives with whom the external field leaders interact and communicate with.

One of the most effective sales teams we have ever seen consisted of professional corporate sales executives from great companies such as Kirby Vacuum and World Book Encyclopedia. These were energetic, disciplined, and highly skilled sales professionals who had the mindset that their job was to serve the volunteer sales force as mentors, trainers, and organizers. Every setting is different though, so be bold and creative when building your sales team.

Take note that, in rare and exciting settings, a field leader may emerge as an excellent candidate to join the internal sales team and bring her knowledge and experience to build the company. However, this is a rare occasion because it takes a unique individual that can do this while holding at bay the jealousies and perceived favoritism that field members may be experiencing. These negative feelings can cause a shift from a collaborative and cohesive team to an envious and hard feeling group.

Sales Presentations

Your best-laid plans will always, always, always require refinement. Don't be discouraged if the first presentation technique for your product or service doesn't win rave reviews on opening night. Careful and thoughtful refinement is the discipline that will pay off.

Make it your top priority to be engaged in as many presentations as possible in the early days of your prelaunch and soft-launch. And establish the practice of debriefing after each presentation so that you can capture the best idea(s) for improving and refining. This truly is a case of "slow and steady wins the race" when it comes to discovering the best presentation techniques for your company's unique mix of products and services.

Party Selling System

The party[6] selling system involves demonstrating and selling products within a personal setting. The key players in this approach include the independent representative, the host, and the guests (the host's friends that were invited to the party).

Successful parties are driven by the desire to be social. Guests come to socialize and have fun, so they're relaxed and often ready to learn about, experience the product, and make a purchase. The dynamics of the group can often even create a "buying frenzy" of sorts. Guests are also motivated to support the host who invited them, knowing she will benefit from their purchases.

---

6   Subsets of parties include home parties, virtual parties, online parties, social media parties, etc.

This is a mature and highly effective selling system that is the primary selling approach of companies such as The Pampered Chef and Scentsy. Network marketing companies also use in-home selling demonstrations, though many don't typically include all the elements discussed here.

There are several advantages to this selling system. From a high-level perspective, companies that use the party model typically grow slower than many of their network marketing counterparts, but they also grow more consistently overtime. In addition, retention of party plan company reps is often double the number of network marketing companies reps.

A party provides independent reps with immediate income through retail sales commissions, making it a very popular approach when households are under pressure for immediate cash and during economic downturns. The party plan rep knows that she can predictably earn cash by doing parties, as opposed to the longer-term income associated with recruiting and building a team of network marketing reps.

Four Objectives of Any Party

A successful party, whether it is online or in-person, will meet four primary objectives: generating sales, booking parties, recruiting independent representatives, and building a customer base for repeat product sales:

- **Selling:** In addition to features, benefits, and pricing of the product, as well as the overall design of the party experience, two important strategies can boost sales at the party: tonight-only specials and closing the party after 24 hours.

  ☐ **Tonight-only Specials:** These are special deals or discounts that are only available in association with the party. Since they are not available anywhere else, they create an urgency to buy at the party. Examples include special product bundles, specific products, discounts for certain purchase amounts, and free shipping.

  ☐ **Close the Party After 24 Hours:** Often, as much as 40 percent of the party volume can come within 24 hours after the official event ends. While we don't recommend that the party stay open for longer than 24 hours, the host can use this time to follow up with invited guests that didn't attend and other friends and relatives who might be interested. By doing this, the host can boost party volume and hit the next level in the host reward program.

- **Booking:** A reliable rule of thumb is that independent reps should try to book two new parties at each party they have. A popular saying in party circles is "empty calendar means empty bank account." As the host reward program is actively publicized during the party and guests connect with the product, the natural result is that guests may wish to book their own parties to capture host rewards for themselves. The independent rep must simply speak up, extend the invitation, and secure commitments.

- **Recruiting:** Another good rule of thumb is that each party should yield one guest who is interested in becoming an independent representative. The independent rep conducting the party should be open with the group about how much she enjoys and benefits from her home-based business, extend the invitation to join her team, and follow up with the prospective reps one-on-one sometime after the party.

The best prospective new team member at each party is the host because the host has had an inside view of what it takes to throw a successful party, as well as how much the rep is making from the party. Hosts may be thinking, "I think I can do this." They just may need some gentle encouragement from the rep.

- **Building a Customer Base:** One of the biggest mistakes made by party plan reps is not effectively building a long-term customer base. If an independent representative conducts two parties a month with an average of ten guests per party, she should end the year with 240 people she's communicating with on an ongoing basis—letting them know about specials, inviting them to host parties, and encouraging them to purchase products from her website. Regardless of whether each guest purchases products at the party, the independent rep should gather each guest's email address or connect with them through social media and gain consent for follow-up communications. Smart companies provide independent representatives with the tools to do this effectively, and they train them to view their parties as only the beginning to a great long-term customer relationship.

Types of Parties

Parties have appeal. Whether the party is in the home of a host, in a meeting room of a hotel, in a restaurant, or other convenient public gathering venue or whether it's a virtual party held through various social media and communications channels, parties are fantastic ways to deliver a social experience that includes food, friends, fun and functional business interaction.

Some parties are less structured such as an open house. For these parties, guests are invited to drop by the host's home anytime during a certain time period to say hello, socialize, and go shopping. There is no structured presentation. This tends to work well for products that don't require demonstration or explanation, such as jewelry. While guests like this approach because it takes less of their time, the logistics of the system (such as signage and effectiveness of the independent rep's interaction with each guest) have to be carefully designed in order for the open house to be successful.

Other parties are more structured and include a start and end time, fun social activities, a brief presentation, and refreshments. To help independent representatives with throwing a party, there is often an event outline and video examples of the ideal party experience included in rep training materials.

In today's world, virtual parties are hugely popular, especially in a society set on high-speed cruise control. These parties allow mothers to put their children to bed and then join the fun of a party online without having to find a babysitter. For students and full-time employees with little time, virtual parties allow them to squeeze in a few minutes to join in on the activities. Interactive tools used in virtual parties make it convenient to comment, respond, ask questions, place orders, or just observe for anyone. In some instances, companies now produce as much as 70 percent to 80 percent of sales through virtual parties.

Choosing which of these approaches is right for your company, product, and independent reps is a strategic decision. Early on, test parties may help you determine which approach you lead with or whether you should use both approaches.

For instance, an apparel company believed that a live "pop-up boutique" where guests try on clothing would be ideal, yet, in a very short time, their Facebook parties replaced 70 percent of the live parties and their attendance grew by as much as five to ten times the previous amount.

Over time, you will observe what works best for your independent reps and build on those successes with your training programs. Regardless of the type of party you select (or a combination of several), these basic principles will help your reps succeed in greater measure:

- **Socializing and Fun:** Many guests view a party as an opportunity to get together with friends, chat, and socialize. Don't over-program the event and be sure to build in time for socializing and making sure guests have fun.

- **Dollar-per-hour Proposition:** Pay attention to the dollar-per-hour proposition associated with time spent and return gained. With measuring and training, reps will eventually learn to exceed the levels of earning with the time that they spend.

- **Complete System:** Provide a complete party system for your reps. As appropriate, supply detailed instructions, forms, signage, electronic tools, and display materials for each step of the event. Wherever exact wording is needed, provide sample scripting. Give reps ideas for activities. Consider producing an overview video that can be used at each party. You might design a "party in a box" that anyone can use, regardless of their background and selling experience.

Host Coaching

Host coaching is a vital part of an effective party. Basic principles are as follows:

- The host must carry out the responsibilities associated with inviting, setting up, supporting the independent rep, and encouraging purchasing and booking.

- A brief host guide should be provided to help each host to be effective. The focus should be on maximizing host rewards.

Host Reward Program

An empty calendar means an empty bank account. While our advanced training provides detailed guidance on booking techniques, the central element associated with booking parties is a competitive host reward program. This gives prospective hosts the motivation to book their own party. Without a competitive host reward program, reps can become discouraged if they're not successful at booking parties.

Your compensation plan designer or our team can help you design your host reward program. While each host reward program is unique, there are some basic principles that are helpful for you to understand:

- Most host reward programs will reward hosts with free and half-price items based on party sales volume.

- A properly designed host reward program is "self-funding"; that is, the profits generated from the half-price items cover the cost of the host rewards for each party.

- In addition to rewarding party sales volume, host reward programs often include rewards for parties booked by attending guests.

- Some host reward programs allow hosts to convert their rewards from the party toward their sign-up costs if they join the independent rep's team as a new rep. The number one recruiting prospect for most party plan reps is the host.

All host programs should include the following rewards:

- **A Thank You Gift:** This gift can be something small that the company or independent representative gives or sells to reps. It should be something the host can use more than once.

- **Product Credit:** It's important for a host to be able to earn free products, not just products priced at a discount. The product credit should be based on a percentage of retail sales made at the party.

- **Half-price Items:** These can be offered when a specific threshold of sales has been met and when bookings are made at the party.

- **Host Specials:** These can be lower margin but highly desirable items. Host specials can be exclusive items only available to hosts, or they can be selected inventory items priced at a discount, or both.

- **A Gift for Hosting a Second Party:** Having an incentive to host two parties will increase the likelihood of a host becoming an independent representative because more hosts decide to become a rep after hosting more than one party.

- **Booking Benefits:** Rewards are offered to the current hosts when guests agree to book their own parties or when the booked parties are held.

Free gifts, host product credit, half-price items, and booking benefits are non-commissionable and are not included in the calculated retail value of the party, nor are upline commissions paid on these items. However, if a host has earned $100 in free product credit and buys a $140 item, then the $40 difference would be commissionable. Host benefits and booking benefits are separate rewards. One cannot apply host credit toward the price of a half-price item.

Your host program should be tailored to fit your product price points and your company's margins. An important secondary goal is to devise the program to be self-funding so that it is at zero cost to the company.

Getting People There

One of the biggest challenges is getting guests to show up at your party. Here are a few tips to help with this challenge:

- **Invitation Systems:** Use multiple means of communication to reach prospective guests. For example, one of the most effective invitation systems we've seen followed these steps:
  - ☐ Contact each prospective guest individually and extend a brief personal invitation.
  - ☐ Send the person a link to a short video that will give a taste of the exciting and fun things that will happen at the party.
  - ☐ Ask them to RSVP after they've watched the video. This process helps avoid your message being ignored or in a spam filter.
  - ☐ Send each guest a message reminding them 24 hours before the party.
  - ☐ Make sure the party is posted on the host's social media page.

As you can see, your process must include multiple touches to be effective in generating interest, excitement, and commitment to attend.

Key Success Metrics

Metrics help company executives target areas for needed improvement. Company averages can be publicized to promote improvement. Key success metrics include:

- Percentage of guests invited who attend
- Percentage of guests attending who purchase
- Total sales volume per party
- Average purchase amount per guest
- Dollar-per-hour income for independent reps
- Number of bookings per party
- Number of recruits per party

Test Parties

As soon as your product is ready, begin conducting test parties. The best-conceived party plan model is always refined and improved over time. Start the process as soon as possible. You can find some of your best, early independent reps through test parties.

Track the key success metrics outlined above and consider including a survey at the end of each test party to find out what guests, hosts, and independent representatives liked and disliked. Foster learning and improvement.

Conclusion

Training your reps to be successful in their selling efforts and providing them with the tools to do so will be of upmost importance for your company. To prepare your company for making successful sales, follow the action steps below.

Essential Action Steps for Launching

- [ ] Identify customer profiles
- [ ] Create host rewards program
- [ ] Design pilot programs and test parties
- [ ] Create training content and learning system
- [ ] Source your sales aids and starter kit

Chapter 4
Compensation Plan

A compensation plan is a part of a motivation strategy. It is an approach designed to help people want to do the things necessary and have the correct behaviors to succeed as an independent representative in your company. Understanding what a good compensation plan is and how to best incorporate it into your company will be key in your success.

Compensation Plan Basics

Your compensation strategy will include three components. Companies that succeed in these three areas win the hearts of their sales force:

- A compensation plan that pays them well for achieving the intended results
- Incentive programs that give them trips, awards, and prizes for their accomplishments
- Recognition that affirms them for succeeding and inspires others to follow their example
- An effective compensation strategy will use all three components in perfect harmony as shown in Figure 4–1.

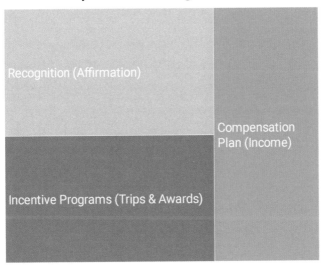

Figure 4–1: Compensation, incentives, and recognition form an overall strategy.

How to Build a Direct Sales Company

A Make-or-Break Proposition

Industry leaders recognize the make-or-break power of a great compensation plan. It often becomes a company's most important piece, whether they are a product focused party plan company or a buying-club network marketing opportunity. Companies who have an effective compensation plan usually enjoy several key benefits:

- Their sales force can recruit effectively
- High retention of new reps builds confidence in the field
- High retention of all levels of leaders builds a strong and continuing commitment and passion among the highest leaders
- Each person knows the time spent selling product generates a predictable income that is worth their time and investment
- Even during difficult times, the business continues to grow, and people keep their passion
- Each dollar spent on commissions and overrides generates a healthy return on investment

Every company would love to enjoy the results listed above and work very hard to achieve them. Unfortunately for most, the results are often elusive, commonly due to flaws in their compensation plan.

Compensation Strategy in the Big Picture

Some think that the compensation plan is the end-all reason behind another company's success. This is not the case. The compensation strategy plays a major part in the success of a company, but not the only part. Other elements of a business model that contribute greatly to the success of a company are:

- Training which builds competence in the field
- A strong and unified management team
- A focus on mission, vision, and values that attracts the passion of others
- A visionary person with whom the field can connect and relate
- Great products offered at competitive prices
- Excellent service provided to the sales force and customers

- Consistent communications with the field
- Effective tools such as kits, forms, and instructional materials
- Simple systems that your sales force use such as web tools, a web order entry system, and reports

In the end, your success depends on many factors all working together, but the most important are illustrated below.

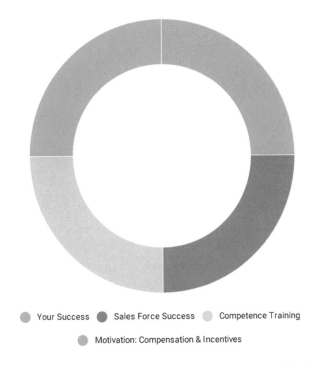

Your Success • Sales Force Success • Competence Training
Motivation: Compensation & Incentives

Figure 4–2: Compensation and incentives must be combined with training in order to create a foundation for true success.

Successful companies quickly learn that motivation isn't enough to build lasting success; they also need good training programs. Motivation without competence doesn't work. Be sure your compensation plan has a strong and effective training program that is in perfect alignment with the principles and techniques for building success.

Designing a Good Compensation Plan

Designing an effective compensation plan is often quite complex. It must sustain low and high growth over many years and motivate people to build successful field businesses. Such a plan is very difficult to design. Unfortunately, most companies find major flaws in their plan designs after their sales force has already developed into leaders that earn significant incomes. Dan Jensen, a respected compensation plan designer and analyst, stated, "Most companies I speak with would change many things in their plan but are so entrenched in their current approach that the thought of changing something makes them run for cover and break out in cold sweat!"

The money you spend to compensate your sales force will most likely be your largest expense category. It is common to pay out 50 percent or more of each retail dollar to one or more of your sales force. Spending the time and money to get your plan "right" the first time will help your business grow and assure you that your top sales force performers are getting the reward they need.

Earnings

Independent representatives are volunteers who work for pay. Their pay is based on performance, and the desired behaviors and results are defined by qualifications with corresponding incentives. There are different kinds of career plans with compensation formulas, but they all have in common certain outcomes that the incentives will drive. For instance, if a company wants all new reps to bring in two more reps within 30 days of their arrival, there will be incentives made such as the award of the first rank (bring in two new reps within 30 days and achieve the rank of "silver" which qualifies you to receive five percent of all purchases made by your recruited reps). In other words, there are different ways to get paid, typically progressive in difficulty, which corresponds to the size of rewards. Below are some of the common categories and types of compensation:

- Commissions based on personal sales of products to consumers, including sales made through the rep's website and/or a customer account tied to the rep's main account
- Commissions paid on the sales volumes of directly and indirectly recruited reps in their sales organizations
- Bonuses paid on achievements such as personal promotions and promotions of others

- Coded bonuses paid specially on pre-determined products and product packs
- Pools allocated to qualified participants based on allocation formulas designed to promote certain behaviors and results

Key Principles of a Successful Compensation Plan

Over the years many compensation plans have followed trends. These have always been short lived. When one company is doing well, others follow their lead and copy their compensation plan. For those who have taken this approach, it has proven fatal. A successful compensation plan is based on proven principles that do not change.

In our 30 years in direct selling, working with hundreds of direct selling companies, we have found that the compensation plans that create the best results follow similar principles of success. If a company gets these principles right, despite a few mistakes in other areas, they will still move forward.

Balancing the Key Sales Force Behaviors

The money spent on sales force compensation represents your single largest expense. The return on investment for this large expenditure must be measured in terms of behaviors. Think about what behaviors you need to build your business and what behaviors you get back from the money you spend on commission. Dan Jensen calls these behaviors the Five Golden Behaviors:

- Retailing
- Recruiting
- Building managers
- Building leaders
- Retention

Exercise: Looking at Your Plan & the Behavior It Supports

There's a simple way to analyze your plan for the behaviors it supports. Take each type of commission at the lowest granular level of detail and ask yourself, "If this was the only type of commission the plan paid, what would it make me do?"

For example, if your plan paid out six percent for four levels of sponsors, isolate the level one commission in your mind. The level one commission engenders two behaviors: recruiting and teaching to sell. Because the behaviors it promotes, your employees would recruit and teach new people in order to be paid.

This would not, however, create managers or leaders, and it would not make the sponsor sell more product (retail profits from personal sales do that). This level one commission plan simply generates recruiting and "teaching to sell" behavior. Now consider what would happen if the plan paid six percent only on level two, instead of level one. What would that make you do? It would encourage you to sponsor members on the first level and then teach those first level employees to recruit and teach others to sell so that you could make a commission when they did.

Go through this mental exercise of isolating each type of commission in your plan and note for each commission type which of the Five Golden Behaviors it creates and fails to create. On Dan Jensen's website (www.danjensen-consulting.com), you can download a "Plan Behavior Analysis Worksheet" that has a template for this type of analytical exercise. When you have looked at each type of commission, see how well your plan addresses all the Five Golden Behaviors. Determine if it is well balanced. Does it spend most of its money on recruiting and very little on building managers and leaders? Or are there other problems? Make a plan to correct these issues.

Building a Strong Retailing Ethic

Of all the Five Golden Behaviors, retailing ethic may have the greatest impact on your success for several reasons:

- DSA statistics suggest that 54 percent of all new recruits were customers before becoming independent representatives. A strong retailing ethic builds sales but creates a pool of great recruiting prospects with your customers.

- Companies with a strong retailing ethic find they can enroll many new customers for every new rep.

- If you want to build a strong retailing ethic, consider these suggestions:

- Build a culture that respects the difference between a retail customer and an independent representative.

- Don't make it too easy to join as an independent representative or you will cut off the profits your independent reps make from retail sales.

- If you are a party plan company, be careful not to encourage your independent reps to aggressively recruit their hosts unless the host really wants to build a business. Some hosts can do more for building sales as a repeat host than they would as an independent representative.

- Have an acceptable retail pricing model. Don't price your products so high that customers get sticker shock. Make it easy for your independent reps to sell at retail.

- Party plan companies should focus on strong booking success in every party. Parties without bookings mean that the seller is out of business.

- Industry wide, most attrition occurs during the first 60 to 90 days as a recruit. Most find that they don't earn enough to justify their time involved. Seventy percent of new recruits do not sponsor even one person in their first 90 days! And very few recruits sponsor two or more. Your compensation strategy must provide a way for your new recruits to make at least $25 to $35 per hour in their first 90 days without a downline otherwise you'll struggle to retain most of your recruits.

Companies that fail to build a strong retail culture become wholesale buying clubs. We refer to this as the internal consumption model of direct selling. If you want strong growth over the long term, build a strong retailing ethic.

Building Strong Recruits

Recruiting is the lifeblood of growth in a direct selling channel. The focus of all recruiting should start with the emphasis on finding customers who can believe in, and benefit from, the inherent value in the company's products, services, business opportunities, and community. Seek those recruits who feel a need for something better (whether product benefits or lifestyle enhancements) and who are willing to make commitments.

The reality is that many who start as customers do not intend to become business builders. As they experience the benefits of the products, the business opportunities, and the company culture, some people become naturally drawn to the idea that the company can be the vehicle for transporting their dreams. The job of a recruiter is to introduce, inspire, instruct, and invite. It's important to not pre-judge a person (whether or not they will be a good customer or a strong recruit) and to believe that the right people at the right time will identify the opportunities in front of them.

The effort that you put into building strong recruits will be to build understanding, to help people identify what inspires them, and to instruct them in the fundamentals so that when they are ready, they will know how to proceed with their personal journey.

Building Strong Managers

To build managers, your compensation plan must have the right incentives that encourage independent reps to become managers. Their income must be well worth the challenge and time commitment. The ultimate goal of a manager is to guide others in their group or team to become strong managers.

Often, we see a culture develop of recruiting bodies as fast as they can. This puts the company on a dangerous path of very high attrition with business builders. In time, such a culture develops an accelerating revolving door, losing many who are coming in. Successful managers believe that every recruit in their group deserves the guidance they need to succeed in the business. Good managers are your future leaders.

Building Strong Leaders

Your success will be found in building a group of strong leaders in the field. Leaders provide the strength that sustains and builds the business over time. To develop a large force of strong sales leaders, keep in mind that all good leaders were strong managers first and that the compensation plan must reward leaders for leadership behavior.

Leadership behavior occurs when employees develop new managers and leaders and help them, in turn, develop other strong managers and leaders. Great leaders hunt for their rising stars below them and mentor them into tomorrow's great leaders. This is how leaders build successful downline organizations. If your plan rewards leadership behavior, you will see a constant stream of new leaders rising to the surface and your business will enjoy long-term health and growth.

Building a Strong Retention Culture

No amount of recruiting will compensate for poor retention. Successful companies quickly learn that retention must become part of their culture of success.

Most attrition occurs very early in the life of a recruit (60–90 days). But how do you keep recruits who have weathered the storms of their first 90 days? How do you keep your leaders and managers from eventually jumping ship?

Here are some tips you'll want your compensation plan to include to help you retain your recruits:

- Use "golden handcuffs" to keep them engaged in the business. Your compensation plan needs to help people develop a recurring income stream as quickly as possible of at least $300 per month. Get early money into the hands of your young reps as quickly as possible. You'll keep them longer.

- Use both a stick and a carrot. Pay them well as they perform but match their earnings to the true level of their performance each month.

- Handsomely reward your strong managers for their team building results. As they work with their team members, you'll see retention increase.

- Your compensation plan needs to carefully balance incentives between personal sales commissions and team building commissions. If you reward managers more for their personal sales than for their team building, you'll see them sell more but fall short in their team building.

- Use recognition at every opportunity to affirm the right behaviors that build successful teams and downline organizations.

Apart from compensation and incentives strategies, companies that successfully retain their managers and leaders find ways to earn the trust of their people. A company that proves to be untrustworthy to their field will find their people leaving. Mistrust trumps a good compensation plan. You must show them that you can be trusted with their precious customers and downline recruits.

Ten Characteristics of a Great Plan

A compensation plan can be compared to a symphony orchestra with several instrumental groups. The woodwinds, brass, percussion, and strings each play a role in creating beautiful music, but only if they are in perfect harmony. Imagine the awful sound if the brass began to play Beethoven's 5th while the woodwinds played a piece from Chopin. To make beautiful music, all the instrumental groups must play a well-composed music score in perfect harmony. In a composition plan, this harmony should create the maximum opportunity for success for every independent rep who wishes to build a long-term business. Whether reps want a fun way to earn a few hundred dollars each month in only a few hours each week or has career aspirations to earn a six-figure, full-time income, the compensation plan must be crafted to help them achieve their dreams.

Be sure that your plan design does everything possible to make each one a reality. Ten foundational principles of a great plan are listed below:

- **Growth Comes Mostly from Retention:** The cost of losing one active independent representative can be measured in hundreds, if not thousands, of dollars over time. Not only do you lose the sales the rep would have generated but also the sales from the recruits she would have recruited and the recruits her recruit would have recruited and so on. In the end, it doesn't matter how many you recruit. What really matters is how many you keep. What benefit does recruiting bring if you lose them as quickly as they join?

- **Each Recruit Deserves All the Help Their Upline Sponsors Can Offer:** When recruits join, they expect to be successful. When those expectations are not met, they leave, usually within their first 90 days. There are many reasons they leave but the main reason generally boils down to them not seeing a compelling enough reason to continue working.

  Learning the business by themselves seldom comes easily to new recruits, and, unless they learn, they will leave. Through the help of their upline sponsors, who have done it before, recruits can learn quickly. Successful business builders learn that every new recruit deserves their time and assistance. In turn, they teach their recruits how to mentor those they will recruit, and so the cycle continues.

- **You Are in the People-building Business:** Personal growth needs to be an essential part of your mission and values, with the compensation plan playing a major role in the process. The plan helps people stretch beyond their natural abilities by enticing people to work harder to move up the career path so they can earn more. While new recruits may feel that they'll never become leaders over hundreds or thousands of others, by helping them progress rank by rank up the career path, eventually they will see that it is reachable. In the process, they gain valuable life skills and improve their personal character and self-esteem step by step.

  Another essential aspect of helping people grow is the strong relationship between the person and their upline. Your compensation plan must reward these relationships extremely well, enticing the super stars of today to help the super stars of tomorrow.

- **Time Is Your Top Competitor:** Independent representatives decide every day where to spend their time. Some days, a rep feels they have "better things to do" than spend time on their business. The compensation plan must be designed to give independent reps, new or experienced, a compelling reason to spend time every day on their business in a balanced fashion. Leaders must learn to spend their time wisely to gain the highest rewards.

- **Reward Those Who Are Actively Engaged:** Your compensation plan must reward those who consistently work in the business and mentor their downline. Like any other form of business, if people stop selling, recruiting, or working with others, their earnings will drop. Some compensation plans continue to pay people their commissions long after they stop working. This is at the expense of those who are working because your business can spend no more than your budgeted amount on commissions (a percentage of sales revenue). The more commissions you pay to those no longer engaged in the business, the less you have to spend on those who continue to work hard.

  Your plan must reward those who are actively engaged in the business month after month. It should not reward well those who spend very little time on their business.

- **The Dream Is Real:** Your compensation plan must pay out enough to the top leaders so that other aspiring leaders will do whatever it takes to achieve the top ranks of leadership as well. "Dream checks" will keep people engaged in the process of advancing up the career path and earning more. If your top leaders do not earn enough to inspire the sales force, you will find few people working hard to achieve top leadership ranks.

- **Train Your Sales Force How to Work the Plan:** No compensation plan can be successful without also providing effective training on how to succeed within the plan. Sales leaders and corporate trainers must reinforce and train the sales force how to "work the plan." There's a difference between understanding "how the plan works" and understanding "how to work the plan." Companies that fail to provide an effective training program for their sales force quickly learn that the compensation plan can never achieve its full impact in generating sales, recruiting, retaining, and building managers and leaders.

- **Help Others Become Successful:** No leader in the direct selling industry has ever become successful without helping others become successful. It has been said, "If you build the people, they will build your business." This exemplifies successful leadership. Leaders who successfully duplicate themselves by mentoring and coaching others in their downline find it much easier to live a balanced lifestyle and smell the roses along the way. They also see their earnings grow exponentially.

- **Develop Successful Managers:** A manager helps and mentors their personal group or unit to sell, recruit, and mentor their personal recruits. Most managers work with 10 to 30 active reps according to their time availability (usually 15–20 hours per week). Success is found when a unit member reaches the same level of competence and becomes a manager of her own unit (promote-out). When this happens, the upline manager should earn more and work with her new manager as a leader and a resource to help the new manager build a stronger downline business. The upline manager continues to see success as the new manager develops other managers. Leaderships skills are learned in this process.

- **Leaders Must Be Rewarded for Leading by Example:** When leaders work with other managers and leaders in their downline to help them develop their groups and their rising stars, they are leading effectively. In this way, people who strive for great success can have many upline mentors (leaders) helping them succeed in their business. These upline leaders must be rewarded for spending time with those committed to building a strong and vibrant business.

  A leader also leads by example. "Do what I do" is the mantra every leader should teach. Those unwilling to lead by example will find their monthly earnings declining because their business will eventually grow weaker. A successful compensation plan asks every leader to be an example of excellence and rewards them well when they are.

Types of Compensation Plans

There are several different types of compensation plans. Being aware of the different types can help you determine what is best for your company.

Unilevel

In direct selling, unilevel means paid solely by level or paid strictly by level. This compensation plan places no limit on the number of independent reps that can be placed in a first-level of downline. Each person in the downline may do the same. This means there will be multiple levels consisting of individuals building their own level.

The number of levels and the percentages earned on the sales volume of independent reps in each level vary based on the qualification of the rep, normally paid on their pay status or pay rank (determined by their current pay qualifications, regardless of the rank they may have previously attained).

Pay title is determined based on a mix of various factors during the commission period such as personal sales volume, group sales volume, number of active personal recruits, number of customers, and total active in downline.

In a unilevel compensation plan, group volume is commonly defined as the personal sales volume of reps in a group. The group can be defined in different ways, often as a specific or varying number of levels of reps. For an illustration of a unilevel compensation see Table 4–1 in the Appendix.

Generation Breakaway

The term breakaway derives itself from the Amway compensation system. It describes what happens when a rep achieves a specific rank in the compensation plan that causes him/her to detach or "break away" from the group he/she belongs to. In the Amway plan, they would then go "direct" to the company, where they would be permitted to purchase directly from the company. The current usage of the term has retained the feature that the rep earns commissions on the sales volumes of his/her group and, based on the paid-as title, they can earn on other groups as well, including other breakaway groups. These bonuses are sometimes referred to as overrides.

Like unilevel plans, most breakaway compensation plans pay independent reps based on their qualifications (paid-as titles) for each commission period. Additionally, as in a unilevel plan, independent reps who are paid through a breakaway compensation plan are not limited to the number of personal recruits placed on the first level of downline.

Breakaway compensation plans begin by paying unilevel commissions or differential commissions. Unilevel commissions are paid based on level relationships, and differential commissions are based on the difference in percentages attributed to each title below the rank of breakaway.

When a rep earns breakaway, the compensation paid to others changes. Some reps who previously earned unilevel commissions may no longer earn them on the downline volume of breakaways. On the other hand, if qualified, they may earn a new percentage on the entire group volume of the breakaway, intended to be a trade-off for helping the breakaway to grow.

In the Appendix, Tables 4–2 and 4–3 show two different breakaway compensation plans, each including overrides.

Forced Matrix

Forced matrix operates within a structure that limits the number of recruits that can be placed in the first level in the downline. With a matrix compensation plan, the upline helps to build the downline.

At Melaleuca, the magic was found in the rank of director being a building block. This required eight active personal recruits placed into a maximum front line with only five positions. This meant that three of the recruits were placed by the sponsor under one or more of the five in their front line. This was leveraged by the smart builders who would use the placement of one of the remaining three as a reward or incentive for others in their group to get their own recruits. In some instances, the sponsor would say, "If you get three recruits, I'll match those with three of mine," and similar recruiting strategies.

It should quickly become apparent that when the first level is full, the sponsor chooses specifically where to place his/her new recruits. Or, in the alternative, the software can be programmed to place the recruit into the first open position (usually as a default).

Compensation in a matrix plan often includes a mix of unilevel commissions that are paid upon a genealogy of actual placement and a mix of commissions or qualifications for the sponsor genealogy. Other variations include compensation on volume produced by personal recruits who have achieved a specific pay rank and variations on generation breakaway paying on group volumes of personal recruits who hit specified achievement goals.

Binary

A binary compensation plan is structurally similar in concept to a two-wide matrix. Yet the method for computing compensation is completely different than in a matrix system. Unlike compensation plans that pay commissions using percentages and sales volumes as the basis for bonuses, binary compensation plans pay threshold commissions based on the accumulation of volumes on the left and right side of a rep's organization.

Compensation is paid to an independent representative when the volume of the lesser leg meets or exceeds specific thresholds (50/50 approach) or when the volume of the lesser leg meets or exceeds two-thirds of specific thresholds (1/3, 2/3 approach).

Active reps with unpaid volumes see their left- and right-side volumes rolled forward to the next commission period. Inactive reps lose the accumulated unpaid volumes. Binary compensation plans count on the occurrence of inactivity, which limits payouts.

The total percentage of compensation paid in a binary compensation plan can vary significantly from one commission run to another. In addition, binaries are famous for creep, the slow but steady increase in the average percentage of compensation paid out in each commission run. Caps or flushing are techniques employed to limit total payout, which is somewhat unpredictable.

Some binary plans allow for the purchase of multiple income centers or the earning of additional income centers based on meeting specific organizational performance criteria. In essence, this serves as a multiplier for earnings.

Hybrid

Hybrid compensation plans are those which incorporate structural elements of more than one plan type. Most compensation plans today are hybrids.

For example, a unilevel generation breakaway hybrid (sometimes called a uni-gen plan) employs elements of both unilevel and generation breakaway compensation plans. A growing number of party plans incorporate multi-level compensation in order to build long-term income based on repeat sales. Conversely, network marketing companies employ party plan presentation elements to gather people in order to demonstrate products but then compensate on a perpetual basis if the products or product lines are well suited for ongoing consumption.

Compression Strategies and Pitfalls

Of all the techniques used to fine-tune a compensation plan, compression is one that is most often used but seldom understood. For many companies, compression is a source of massive waste in their compensation plan—dollars being spent with little return. When done correctly however, it is a source of focused and well-planned incentives on independent rep performance, which is otherwise difficult to obtain.

Compression Defined

In network marketing, compression and roll up are terms that are often used interchangeably; however, we like to use the term compression. Compression can be defined as the impact on a business genealogy when an independent representative account is terminated. The downline of the terminated rep account is linked to the sponsor of the terminated rep causing a "compression" effect on the downline.

When commissions are calculated, the computer attempts to pay a commission on the purchase of each downline rep to each of their qualified upline sponsors. Commissions are always paid upline by special programming that determines who is qualified to be paid and which orders and volumes are to be paid.

Commission compression happens if a commission on the purchase or sale by a downline rep cannot be paid to an upline sponsor due to that sponsor being unqualified. The commission will then "compress" to the next upline qualified sponsor, provided this is a feature in the compensation plan design.

For example, a simple unilevel plan pays 10 percent from level one and 10 percent from level two but only if the independent rep purchases $100 in the month (see Figure 4–3 below).

Compression has a significant effect on the commission A. Without compression, A receives a level one commission from B's $100 purchase. A does not receive a level two commission from C because C purchased nothing. A does not receive commission from D because D is at level three, beyond the reach of A.

With compression, A receives $10 from B, nothing from C (no purchase volume), and, for this month only (next month C may be active, again), D is counted as second level to A, so A receives 10 percent on D's $100 purchase. Conceptually, A receives commissions on two active levels with compression and, therefore, reaches deeper, ignoring inactive reps when counting levels.

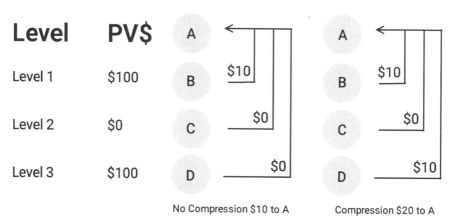

Level	PV$		
Level 1	$100		
Level 2	$0		
Level 3	$100		

Figure 4–3: Compression example.

Why Offer Compression?

A golden rule of compensation plan design is to apply the compensation dollars toward the behavior that is desired. Compression can encourage positive behaviors by helping sales leaders work deeply in their downline and enticing sales leaders to move up the ranks by reaching deeper.

Compression can be a tremendous incentive for your active sales leaders who have large downlines. If you are giving away compression commissions to non-producers, to the less active, or to those with shallow downlines, consider making changes to your plan.

Common Mistakes

These are four common mistakes to avoid when using compression:

- **Mistake #1:** Offering compression to all independent representatives. Many plans we have seen offer compression to all independent representatives as if it would turn on a huge amount of additional performance across the board. This is not so. Compression works most effectively with sales leaders who have large organizations. It offers little incentive for reps with shallow organizations.

- **Mistake #2:** My competitors do it, so I should too. Don't fall into the trap of doing it just because others do it. Do it because it's right for you. Compression costs your competitors a lot of money, which could be put into other parts of the plan to get higher returns, such as starting with specific, desired rep behavior.

- **Mistake #3:** Giving compression to non-producers. Understanding what behavior is rewarded with compression, it becomes apparent that it should focus on qualified and performing sales leaders. Giving compression to poorly performing reps should be considered a waste of precious incentive dollars.

- **Mistake #4:** Not budgeting for compression. Compression is expensive because it almost always pays out to the maximum limit of the plan. Without compression, the company retains breakage to a much larger degree. Plans with compression should expect to pay out close to their theoretical maximum.

Dollar-per-hour Proposition

Perhaps you have tried everything to motivate your sales force, but sales are still not climbing. Each incentive program seems to see a small bump in sales and recruiting, but, as soon as the incentive is over, you're back to a flat-line trend. You wonder if your compensation plan needs to be fixed. Your leaders are frustrated. People aren't moving up the career path like they used to. Your seasoned independent reps don't seem to have the passion you saw a few years ago. What's wrong? What's at the root of the problem? Read on and you may discover the secret to unlocking the door to sustainable growth. We call it the dollar-per-hour proposition.

Problems with Keeping Recruits

The attrition rate for new independent representatives during their first year is very high. While we are unaware of any published data on this, our experience suggests that an average of 80 percent of our new recruits fall away within their first 12 months. The majority leaves during their first 90 days. Yet, we know a few companies whose attrition rate is less than 20 percent. How do they do it? How does a company keep 80 percent of their recruits during the first 12 months?

To answer these questions, we must first recognize another uncomfortable truth: most recruits in their first 90 days do not sponsor even one person. Perhaps they are afraid. Perhaps they don't feel they know enough yet to bring a new recruit into the business. Whatever their reason, for the most part, it doesn't happen. That leaves us with a big challenge. How can we give them a compelling reason to spend time on the business during their first 90 days? Most don't even have a downline from whom they can earn even a small commission?

If they do sponsor one or two people, what will their first few commission checks be? Imagine the excitement when after weeks of working her business, Suzy opens her first commission check for $8.75! Companies that rely solely on downline commissions to persuade their new recruits to spend time on the business inevitably see their attrition rate rocket to dizzying heights.

How Much Is Compelling Enough?

What is compelling enough for recruits to stay may be different for each rep. Our experience suggests that companies whose reps earn about $25 per hour or more keep a much higher percentage of their sales people and have consistent growth. Knowing that each rep will be exposed to frequent rejection and negative comments from spouses and friends (honey, why don't you get a real job?), we must offer more than other part-time options available. The nature of direct selling is that it has no schedule, no structure, and, usually, no real supervision to help a person succeed.

Most people feel very uncomfortable when put into an environment where there are no clear expectations, no scheduled working hours, and no boss to correct you when you make a mistake. Direct selling is a tough job, no matter how you slice it. If we don't provide a compelling offer for their time, we will continue to see our recruits leaving for other part-time options. A waitress at a restaurant, with tips, can earn $15 to $20 per hour. Our compelling offer must be better than this. Much better.

While our independent reps usually don't calculate what their dollar-per-hour rate is, they feel it, they sense it, and they always know when they aren't getting enough for their time. With such a high percentage of women in this business, their husbands ask the same question: is it worth our time for her to do this business? How many women have left the business because they didn't receive the support they needed? How different the story would have been in many cases had she been earning $25 to $35 per hour? We have seen many husbands become "believers" when their wives are consistently making $25 per hour or more. In some cases, in fact, they are pushing them out the door to do more!

Consider also how much passion a rep would need to recruit their friends and neighbors if they are only making $10 per hour. "Sallie, come join me and you can earn $10 per hour just like me!" Not very inspiring, is it? Imagine, however, if the rep is earning $35 per hour. "Sallie, I'm making loads of money in my business, and it's easy to learn how. Come and join my team!" What a difference it makes to know that your recruit will earn enough to make it worth their time.

If It's Well Below $25 Per Hour

Companies that fall below $25 per hour often find that their compensation plan fails to capture the attention and passion of most of their sales force. In other words, "until I can make decent money in this business, I am not going to share the opportunity with my friends." And why should they? When your dollar-per-hour proposition is poor, we usually see the following happen:

- Recruiting and passion for opportunity is poor
- Attrition is high
- Few people advance in the career path to become leaders
- Business builders burn out because their recruits leave

- Sales will climb for a while and then plateau
- Your leaders start looking for other opportunities

We know a company that after two years in business and hundreds of independent reps joining them has achieved a 90 percent retention rate. They have found the secret. Their reps, both young and experienced, are usually making more than $100 per hour doing parties. Who wouldn't want to walk away with $100 per hour? This is a huge contrast to another company we know that has less than a $10-per-hour proposition. Their attrition rate is 99 percent per year.

If you find yourself staring at flat sales and recruitment charts, look closely at your dollar-per-hour proposition. You can always find things that will improve your dollar-per-hour proposition and deliver a compelling reason for people to spend time on the business.

When determining what affects your dollar-per-hour proposition consider these three major factors:

- Average time per presentation (one-on-one or party)
- Average sales volume per presentation
- Average costs to the independent rep for each presentation

Once you improve these factors, your sales will climb.

Using the Power of a Proven System

There is a reason that party plans work, and why first-year party plan retention is double that of first-year network marketing. Much can be learned by borrowing from the power of a proven system of the party plan model.

You could incorporate some of this process into your network marketing. What about one-on-one network marketing selling? Follow a similar approach for an individual sales presentation, but you will also need to add in a few other factors. Network marketing companies that are able to employ an auto-ship program should factor in an average revenue per independent rep or customer into the model recognizing typical attrition rates. For example, if an average auto-ship customer lasts six months at $50 per month, this would add $300 to the average sales amount.

Compensation Plan Definitions

These are some of the most common compensation plan definitions for you to be aware of:

- **Accumulated Group Volume (AGV):** A rep's group volume from the day he or she becomes a rep until the present. This value does not clear or reset each commission period; it continues to grow.

- **Accumulated Personal Volume (APV):** A rep's personal volume from the day he or she becomes a rep until the present. This value does not clear or reset each commission period; it continues to grow.

- **Active:** Reps are considered active when they meet the minimum requirement for personal volume and/or group volume. Some plans impose other requirements as well. Only active reps may have earnings.

- **Back End:** A term used to describe the portion of a step-level/breakaway plan which pays commissions to breakaway reps. (See *Front End*)

- **Bonus Volume (BV):** The qualifying volume from the sales order that will be the volume credited for a sale. It is added to the personal and group volume of the purchasing rep and the group volume of upline reps according to the plan. This volume may optionally be different than the volume on which the commissions are paid. (See *Commissionable Volume*)

- **Breakage:** Many reps are either unqualified or ineligible to receive some or all types of commission each month. When the company retains these unpaid commissions, they are called breakage. Breakage also happens when an order is placed by a rep who is close to the top of the genealogy, such as a rep sponsored directly by the company. In these cases, the company retains some or all of the commissions that would normally be paid to an upline because there are few, if any, reps in the purchaser's upline. The commissions are always paid upline. When the upline is small or nonexistent, the company retains the unpaid commissions, causing breakage.

- **Breakaway:** When reps are promoted to a certain title, they "break away" from their sponsors and are thereafter called breakaway reps. Their group volume is no longer included in their sponsor's group volume. Breakaways are entitled to additional compensation, which is usually referred to as a generation override. Breakaway positions are usually considered sales leaders.

- **Commissionable Volume (CV):** The assigned value of each purchased product on which commissions are paid. It is in the currency of the country in which the order was placed (though the eventual commission check may be issued in yet a different currency). Sales aids usually have no commissionable value. Commissionable products have a commissionable value, which does not have to equal the price paid for the product.

- **Commissions:** An amount paid to a rep on his or her direct and downline commissionable volume. It usually comprises commissionable volume within his own group. Some plans call all forms of payment to reps a commission.

- **Compression:** Used to describe the impact on a genealogy when a rep is terminated. In this case, the downline of the terminated rep is linked to the sponsor of the terminated rep causing a "compression" effect on the downline.

- **Downline:** The rep personally sponsored by a rep, as well as all the rep they sponsor and so on. For example, you sponsor Jim, who sponsors Mary, who sponsors Ted are all in your downline.

- **Enrolling Sponsor:** The sponsor who recruits a new rep or customer. This person may be different from the sponsor assigned to the new recruit in some compensation plans such as matrix or binary plans. It may be different if a rep's enrolling sponsor is terminated. In this case, the rep is placed under the terminated rep's sponsor. (See *Sponsor* and *Compression*)

- **Exemptions:** Reps may be permanently or temporarily exempted from meeting certain requirements for qualification. These should be clearly defined but not published. Reps should not expect to be exempted when they fail to meet their qualifications, even when they have an excuse. Reality requires the capability, however, to deal with corporate mistakes and other exceptions.

- **Front End:** A term used to describe the portion of a step-level/breakaway plan which pays commissions to non-breakaway reps. (See *Back End*)

- **Genealogy:** The sales organization of a company or rep. It is also called a downline.

- **Generation:** The relationship between an upline breakaway and a downline breakaway, not including non-breakaways. The first breakaway in a leg is a first-generation breakaway. Generations are counted based on this period's fully qualified title.

- **Generation Override:** The commissions paid to upline generations based on group volume.

- **Group:** All downline reps not including any other breakaway rep or the groups of other breakaways.

- **Group Volume (GV):** The total of all personal volume (PV) sold by a group for a commission period. This includes one's own PV.

- **Inactive:** Each commission period that a rep is not active is considered inactive.

- **Leg:** Each personally sponsored rep and all his or her downline. Also referred to as line of sponsorship.

- **Level:** The position a rep has in a downline relative to an upline rep. Reps personally sponsored are level one to the sponsor. Those reps sponsored by level one reps are level two, relative to the original rep. (See *Qualified Level*)

- **Level Override:** The commissions paid upline reps based on relative position in the genealogy. Note this is only paid to qualified levels. This type of commission is usually paid only in unilevel compensation plans, not step-level/breakaway plans.

- **Orphan:** When a new rep joins a company, a rep application form is completed and sent to the company. On the application, the new rep's sponsor name and account number is noted so the company can link the new rep to his sponsor. Occasionally, the sponsoring rep noted on the application is incorrect or nonexistent making it impossible to correctly link a new rep to an existing sponsor. In such cases, the rep is called an orphan. Resolving orphan-sponsor linkages quickly is a high priority with most companies to avoid problems caused by not paying commissions to the correct upline.

- **Paid-as Title:** The title a rep is qualified for in each commission period. This title is not necessarily the rep's permanent title and it may change with each commission run but the title does not. The paid-as title can't be greater than the permanent title.

- **Personal Volume: (PV):** Personal volume is the value of commissionable products purchased in a commission. It is based on the sum of each purchased product's qualifying volume, credited to one purchasing rep in a commission period, represents the total value of commissionable product purchased and usually included in the rep's group volume. When retail customers buy directly from the company, the qualifying volume of their order is usually included in the personal volume and group volume of their sponsoring rep.

- **Qualifying Volume (QV):** The value of a commissionable product which is applied toward rep qualifications in the compensation plan. This value is added to both personal volume and group volume when purchased. It is different than commissionable volume. Commissionable products have a qualifying volume, which does not have to equal the price paid for the product. (See *Commissionable Volume*)

- **Qualified:** In most plans, a rep is qualified if they can receive generation overrides.

- **Qualified Level:** Some unilevel plans which pay commissions based on levels instead of rank or title pay based on qualified levels. In these plans, a qualified level is represented by each qualified rep in a single leg or single chain of reps. Inactive reps are not counted as qualified levels in these plans.

- **Recruit:** A rep who is recruited by another rep to participate in the compensation plan or business opportunity.

- **Retail Volume:** The total retail value of commissionable products is called retail volume. Retail volume is seldom used by compensation plans; most plans rely on wholesale values to determine qualifying and commissionable volumes used in their compensation plan.

- **Sponsor:** The rep immediately upline of a rep. It is usually the person who originally recruited the rep but may be different if the sponsor has inherited one or more people through compression due to the termination of previously sponsored rep. This may be different in other plans such as in matrix or binary plans. In these plans it is common for the sponsor to be different from the original enrolling sponsor. (See *Enrolling Sponsor*)

- **Stacking:** A usually undesirable technique used by reps to manipulate the compensation plan. Stacking occurs when a rep recruits other reps placing them in a single downline leg or chain instead of directly under the recruiting rep.

- **Unencumbered Group Volume (UGV):** To avoid the group volume of one rep inadvertently promoting his sponsor (and his sponsor and so on), some plans require group volume, used for advancement to breakaway position, to be derived from sources other new breakaway reps. These sources are often other legs within the group, ones not being advanced to breakaway positions. The group volume derived from these sources is considered unencumbered volume. This distinguishes it from the group volume used by a downline rep that breaks away. (See *Stacking*)

- **Upline:** A rep's sponsor, along with his or her sponsor and so on. All independent reps in the genealogy above another rep are referred to as the rep's upline. For example, if A sponsors B who sponsors C who sponsors D, then the upline of D consists of A, B, and C.

Conclusion

A compensation plan is an important piece to the success of your company. Don't let it go overlooked and avoid starting with a weak one. Start out right by following the action steps presented below.

Essential Action Steps for Launching

- ☐ Design your compensation plan and rep career path
- ☐ Create your compensation plan presentation
- ☐ Write the compensation plan programming specifications
- ☐ Program and test the compensation plan

Chapter 5
Marketing & Branding

A common business philosophy declares that it is best to be first in the marketplace, but we believe it is better to be first in the prospect's mind than first in the marketplace. This is especially true when prospects first hear of your company and product from you or your independent reps. Being first in the marketplace is important only if it allows you to get in the prospect's mind first. Knowing what kind of view prospects have and what kind of view you want them to have of your company will help you determine what is the best kind of marketing and branding to use. Getting your idea or concept within a prospect's mind is the work that lies ahead of you.

Positioning Your Company

If you want to make a big impression on someone, you can't worm your way into their mind and then slowly build up a favorable opinion over time. The mind doesn't work that way. Once they perceive you one way, that's it. They don't like to change their minds, so you have to "blast" your way into their mind.

Think of the mind as a vast plot of real estate that is claimed and developed by marketers. Once you claim and develop a parcel (however small or large), it is a permanent development. The most powerful work meetings we have with start-up companies are the day-long discussions explaining how that mental real estate will be developed. We cover questions such as:

- What are you offering people?
- What are you really offering? At the end of the day, how is the person better off with your product?
- Why will they buy your product from you and not from someone else?
- If the consumer already has something that fills that need, why

will they change? If it's a new category, how will you get frugal families to justify spending the extra dollars?

- Is there already something in that "mental real estate?" What is it, and what is its value?

- Does the value hold up under critical circumstances? If there is no business opportunity associated with this good or service, does the value diminish? If so, by how much?

This fundamental strategy of getting an idea or concept into the prospect's mind frequently causes would-be entrepreneurs to stumble. In the end, the energy and resources you put into correctly understanding and positioning your company will be the genesis of your success. Once it is correctly and clearly defined, then the growth and magic can begin to happen.

Image and Branding Strategies

You can significantly increase your success if you find a way to plant a single word in the prospect's mind. Not a complicated word, not an invented one, but a simple word taken right out of the dictionary.

You "blast" your way into the mind by narrowing the focus to a single word or concept. For example, if the given words are overnight, chocolate bar, and pink Cadillac, the companies that come to mind are Federal Express, Hershey's, and Mary Kay.

Isolate your product's most important attribute. For example, in 1968, Heinz Ketchup claimed leadership on the thickness attribute as the "Slowest Ketchup in the West." Owning the word slow in people's minds helped Heinz maintain a 50 percent market share. If you can't be a market leader (such as The Pampered Chef being the top in kitchen parties), then your word must have a narrow focus that no one else has locked in.

Your branding strategies should reflect the image you wish to convey, the words and concepts you claim, and the mental real estate you'll develop in people's minds. A logo, brand, tag line, style guide, and so forth, all help create a "handle" people can grab onto when they are reaching for something to buy. As you work on your image and branding strategies, it is important to know your brand strategy, have a simple brand idea, and have branding signals. Consider the example below of how this may be done.

Example: JetBlue Airlines Branding Strategy

When considering their brand strategy, simple brand idea, and branding signals, JetBlue Airlines might make this list for their personal brand:

- **Brand Strategy:** To signal that the experience of flying JetBlue is more enjoyable than any other airline experience
- **Simple Brand Idea:** Flying can be fun
- **Branding Signals:** Very pleasing employees, in-flight entertainment, user-friendly website, interesting choice of snack food

This branding strategy reflects the image of flying with JetBlue being fun and pleasant. When people are considering who to fly with, JetBlue's image of being fun and pleasant can be the driving reason for why people would choose to fly with them.

Selecting Primary Products or Services

Not all products sold through direct selling channels are tangible ones. Direct selling companies also offer services such as financial services, investments, insurance, travel, security systems, legal services, telecommunications, utilities, and more.

The most successful direct selling products are those that don't sell well unless they are explained. Retail is simply not an effective channel for moving this kind of merchandise or services.

Key considerations in selecting products and services include:

- Uniqueness that isn't likely to change rapidly
- Exclusivity that is protected either by trade secrets or legal protections such as patents
- Ability to stay in front of product development, innovations, and refinements
- Unique or special qualifications of a business owner, inventor, scientist, etc.

Determining the need that a product or service will fulfill is the first step in selecting what to offer. To do this, answer these questions:

- What is the inherent potential in the product? Is it something people need?
- What are the features and benefits of the product or service?
- How broad is the public appeal likely to be?
- Who will buy and use the product or service?
- Is it easy to target your market for this product or service?
- Can you identify the men and women who will use the product?
- Can it be sold at a reasonable price?
- Will margins meet our requirements for sufficient commissions and company profits?

Finding and acquiring products is the second step in selecting what to offer. This requires answering questions such as:

- Can you manufacture the product?
- Are key ingredients easily available or in limited or restricted supply?
- Are the rights or formulas protected and exclusive?
- Are distribution rights available and exclusive?
- Does due diligence return green lights, yellow lights, or red lights?

Line Extensions

It may be wise to launch a single product and expand later. Remember the wisdom of positioning, mental real estate, and one-word dominance. Companies often create the most interest by offering a single product or a single group of products, and then expand naturally in response to more of a demand.

However, once you have a good following, you have to be careful that you don't ruin a good thing. Our fellow direct selling consultants are misguided when they suggest that a single highly profitable and widely accepted product is a sign that it's time to launch extensions.

When you try to become everything to everyone, you wind up in trouble. You run high risks when you start tinkering with a successful formula. Remember that marketing is a battle of perception, not products, so consider carefully what line extensions will do to the goodwill you built with your lead product(s) and service(s). The leader in any product or service category is the brand that is not "line extended."

For too many companies, line extensions become the hope of new momentum. There are razor-sharp strategies that support and have proven line extension theories, and we fully support these when they are carefully researched. However, owners or management teams often get bored (despite the sheer insanity of fast growth) or greedy and move to the easy way out—line extensions—without giving proper planning and research about "what's next?"

Pricing Strategies

Pricing your products can be one of the most challenging things you'll do. Theoretically, the price of every item you carry should cover the cost, the freight charges, a fair share of overhead, and the commissions while still yielding a reasonable profit. In reality, some items bring a high gross profit while others bring in low or no gross profit. As long as the aggregate gross and net profit are sufficient, your business will be successful.

These questions are useful to consider when you are setting up your pricing strategies:

- What are your known percentages (cost of goods, commissions, overhead, and EBITDA[7] objectives)?

- How unique or exclusive are the products or services, and what are the products or services a person would buy instead of yours? How are they priced in comparison?

- What unique packaging strategies exist to differentiate from others? (Are you packaging your powdered nutrition for bottled water in foil sticks and standard boxes—like other off-the-shelf products? What alternatives are you considering, such as square packets in round boxes?)

Price is only one factor in creating pricing strategies. Don't market a low price unless the product and pricing analysis demands it. Walmart

---

7 EBITDA = earnings before interest, taxes, depreciation, and amortization.

plays the pricing game, but The Pampered Chef doesn't have to.

Make sure the features and benefits are strong. Our retention research shows that people who quit buying because "the products cost too much" are really saying they don't understand the value. This means that they have forgotten, or they never really understood, the true features and benefits of the products or services.

Another thing to keep in mind is that peer pressure is a beautiful thing in a home party setting. The ambiance, setting, and focused display of a product can set it apart in the mind of the shopper who is not comparison shopping and who is in an entirely different setting than in the price-driven retail environment.

Merchandising

To be an attractive business you must have value in:

- Product/service
- Brand
- Opportunity and earnings

If you deliver at least two of these values, then retention will skyrocket. On the other hand, if you deliver only one of the values, then attrition rates can become high. The goal in enrollment is getting people to join and stay.

The DSA reports fewer than 20 percent of independent reps stay because they are making enough money. You can secure your reps by building their belief in the company through branding. Immediately after enrollment, reps must start showcasing the brand with business cards, apparel, etc.

Print and apparel is the perfect "add-on" and "upsell." This is a commonly overlooked profit center. We recommend taking advantage of every opportunity to remind your independent reps of your store and highlighted products in it. Some ideas of ways to reach your reps are:

- Enrollment packages
- Links from your website
- Links in member areas

- Flyers in monthly shipments, monthly newsletters, and emails
- Blogs, discussion boards, and forums
- Phone upselling

Things to Consider If You Do It Yourself

It is a common practice to outsource when making merchandise. However, if you are creating your merchandise yourself, consider these factors:

- The true cost of apparel (shirts, hats, etc.):
  - ☐ Inventory purchase (maintaining levels, etc.)
  - ☐ Warehouse use
  - ☐ Order fulfilment
- The cost of printed materials (business cards, fliers, etc.)
  - ☐ Order receipts
  - ☐ Graphic design changes/personalization
  - ☐ Production and shipping

Brochures, Catalogs, and Rep Materials

Stationery and supplies are a reflection of your business. Choose them carefully. Creating a company logo that will represent your company in letterheads, business cards, envelopes, signage, literature, logo merchandise, and web design is a heavy responsibility.

If you have sufficient artistic skill, you may want to create the logo and style guide yourself. If you do not have the skill, hire a designer or graphic artist to create the logo and style guide for you. We are happy to refer the time-tested pros that do great work. Although the cost will vary from region to region, services generally range from $1,000 to $3,500. You can request camera-ready formats as well as the common array of digital formats for various uses.

Be sure to have your designer use common law trademark or service mark ("™" or "SM") designations unless your logo is registered with the U.S. Patent and Trademark Office, in which case you will use the symbol for registered trademark, "®."

Be sure to use a local printer or seek out reliable online printing services. You'll want to have a provider who can present you with an online template for all independent reps to use and who can fulfill business card and stationery orders placed directly by reps. It's quite common for a company to simply negotiate for a percentage of each purchase, which the printer builds into the pricing structure.

In determining which brochures and materials to use, we can provide you with our workshop section that guides you through organizing the plan for designing logos, websites, DVDs, CDs, independent representative manuals, brochures, mailers, packaging, labels, core design elements, etc.

Video and Audio Production

Direct selling is relationship selling and this is best done through stories. Video and audio are both affordable and effective media for storytelling. Some of the most effective ways to use this tool in direct selling include:

- Introduction to the company, products, and/or business stories
- Testimonials
- Staff training and certification
- Independent representative training and certification
- Independent representative "fast start" and orientation
- President's message or video newsletter
- Establishing/reinforcing leadership and culture

Selecting video and audio production support should include close attention to cameras and photographers, sound studios (local and remote), writing, directing, technology such as teleprompters, lighting, and editing/post-production support. Video can effectively tell stories when they are carefully and responsibly scripted and consistently told.

Web Marketing

If businesses do not have control of their brand or image, then their products or services become commodities and are only purchased based on best price. Is that how you want to be valued? It is important that all your branding and marketing efforts are working together with the same message rather than independent fragments of information that could confuse customers and frustrate recruitment efforts. Many competitors try to siphon away your business by appearing as or mimicking your business when it is searched online.

It is important to realize that there are many new and powerful tools available on the internet. Not maximizing every available online resource is a missed opportunity to showcase what is unique about your company and to drive in new business and new rep recruitment.

Using your internet resources will help you establish and promote brands and recruit and retain reps. The internet has changed the ways that we interact with each other and how we do business.

These days, you can find virtually anything online. Word-of-mouth referrals are mostly invitations for us to research online. When you recommend your favorite vacation spot to your friends and promise that they will have the time of their lives, chances are they'll thank you and then research it online.

The same applies when potential reps evaluate your business opportunity versus the hundreds of other similar companies that you are competing against. They'll go online when considering if the opportunity is unique or the best opportunity for them. If they truly believe that your products are valuable to them or that you offer an opportunity to be part of something unique, then they will be willing to pay more and fight harder to get the new business to work.

Your Image Online

As you embrace the internet, the real question is: "When potential reps are searching, are you really in control of your image and is your voice truly there to tell your unique story?"

Today, the internet is flooded with information that frustrates searchers and misdirects them with clever titles or eye-catching images. If you want to capture interest and drive people to your business, your information must be clear and understandable. You also need to stay current with the times. The internet is constantly evolving and changing technologies, so it is no longer enough to have just one website.

You must also be sure that your unique content is located on the first page of a Google search. Spending money on just one website with no consideration for the rest of the search results page would be like spending money to dress up the interior of a home without being concerned about its location in the middle of the ghetto. Your home would be instantly devalued when only looked on the outside.

Today you must own multiple, varied search results that fill and protect your online real estate. Information is constantly being uploaded to the internet. There is no editorial review or truth detector online. If you don't put your name and accurate information out there, no one will find your business.

It is not only important to create multiple search results but also to manage those results and promote each of them in a way that tethers them all together in promoting your company's image and products. Fill the entire Google search results page with your own controlled content to showcase your services, unique opportunities you provide, charity work, community involvement, business awards, etc. Keep in mind that the number of bloggers rating and scoring people and businesses are on the rise. Don't leave it up to them to determine what people read about you.

Social Media

Does it really matter if you have social sites for your business? If properly managed and promoted, social media can be a very powerful marketing tool to develop a relationship directly with your independent reps and their networks and to share information. Don't just create a Facebook or Twitter account because you heard it would be good.

These sites are a vehicle to find "friends" or "followers" who want to stay up-to-date on the latest tips, coupons, contests, giveaways, news updates, new products releases, exciting new trips, and so on. The more exciting and valuable information you share, the more interest you will generate for your business.

Conclusion

Your ability to plant your intended image or concept into a prospect's mind will be the main focus behind your marketing and branding plan. This important strategy will make all the difference. Complete the checklist below to keep up with the essential tasks you will need to succeed.

Essential Action Steps for Launching

- ☐ Position your company
- ☐ Design your image and create your branding strategies
- ☐ Select your primary products
- ☐ Set your pricing strategies
- ☐ Secure URLs
- ☐ Create your website
- ☐ Set up your company's merchandising system
- ☐ Create product catalog, brochures, videos, and literature

Chapter 6
Independent Rep Training & Development

A successful business requires independent representatives who know what they are doing. Because of this, training and developing your independent reps to be capable in their task should be of top importance to you. Businesses without trained reps result in low attrition rates and forces of inadequate reps who lack confidence in what they are doing.

New Independent Rep Training

A new recruit's excitement dissipates within the first 72 hours of signing up, and they may begin to doubt their decision. You must do all you can to reassure them they that they made the right choice. Beginning with new independent representative orientation is crucial to doing this.

Field Training System

In any business, training and management are keys to success, but, in direct selling and network marketing companies, they are more than that. Field training and development comprise the fuel that propels your organization forward.

We have created an approach called Fast Start to evaluate and create or upgrade the field training system for a billion-dollar client. This tool focuses on the training and support that should happen during a new independent representative and customer's opening hours and days.

There are four topics covered in the Fast Start module:

- Market segmentation which establishes a framework for assigning training topics and methods to appropriate independent representatives and customers

- Team retention which focuses on the responsibilities of the independent representatives to lead and train one another

- Contact tracking which identifies recurring issues in an effort to improve (improvement comes from system upgrade, staff, and field training)
- Field surveys which pinpoint expectations, desires, needs, and problems associated with motivation and ability

Training and development systems must be tied to specific needs at each phase of an independent rep's time in your company, beginning with their very first exposure to your company. At the heart of retention is expectations, and, therefore, expectation must also be at the heart of training.

Know what your reps' and customers' expectations are, how to attain these expectations, and what training and development is needed to perform this task well. Fast Start examines the essentials behind effective field training and development in direct selling.

Objectives

For you to be most effective, remember that you are devoting time and energy to improve retention in the field.

Paul Timm, retired professor of organizational leadership and strategy at Brigham Young University, points out that the cost of obtaining a new customer is six times the cost of retaining an existing one (Career Press, Hawthorne, New Jersey). He believes that satisfied customers are the best advertising.

In support of that point, at Mary Kay, it was noted that obtaining a new customer costs five times more than maintaining an existing customer.

In the same vein, two critical statistics were noted at Mary Kay relating to an independent rep's first year. First, it was discovered that the majority of terminations occur during the first year, and as many as 40 percent of those occur in the first 90 days. Second, it was found that independent reps bring in the highest numbers of new recruits during their first year. In short, new reps are highly important to the sales organization, yet they are the most likely to drop out of the program.

With these points in mind, here are some objectives that should be focused on in field training and development:

- Help new customers and reps get off to a fast and strong start
- Get your reps and their customers past their 90-day and first-year hurdles
- Develop a deep sense of value around your products and programs
- Impart the information and skills required by reps and their customers
- Forge a bond of trust and loyalty that will withstand the forces of attrition
- Establish a reliable channel for communicating your culture, energy, and important enhancements
- Motivate and inspire your reps
- Provide fresh insights and success secrets
- Develop leaders who are knowledgeable, passionate, and confident

Foundation for Training Systems

There are the five foundational principles that should guide the successful development of your training systems:

- **Retention:** Education and training should measurably increase attraction and retention of independent reps and customers and should be developed with that goal in mind. These measures determine the true success of an effective training and education program.

  Over a 15-year period, we studied more than 100 companies in search of the secrets of retention. Out of 112 companies, 16 proactively sought to improve retention of customers and independent reps. Of those 16, four had achieved retention rates of 70 percent or better per year.8 With their help, we identified the powerful principles of retention and the best practices that the retention leaders used. Five disciplines of the high-retention companies that

---

8   The 1997 DSA and 1998 Wirthlin studies, independently concluded that the annual retention rate of direct sales and network marketing companies averages 20 percent per year with 80 percent attrition.

stood out in the study include discipline of routine, specific measurements that show the impact and return on investment (ROI) of training, education, recognition, and other retention-focused initiatives.

- **Customers and Independent Reps:** Customers and independent reps enroll with the company for different reasons. They also come with different needs, which should be carefully considered when training and educating reps. Many of their needs will overlap, inviting common training elements to be able to serve multiple needs. However, where their needs are different and unique, training and education should be distinct and separate. Thus, your training systems will likely include separate (but related) training programs.

- **Life Cycle:** The life cycles of customers and independent reps have distinct, measurable phases that occur in various categories of activity. Training content and delivery methodologies must be matched to specific needs at each phase of a life cycle, beginning immediately upon enrollment. Additionally, pre-enrollment considerations must be woven into the design of the training and education system. For example, the following illustration shows the basic life cycle of a customer or independent representative.

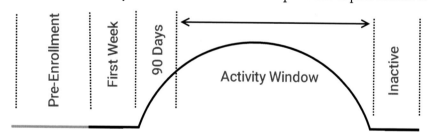

Figure 6–1: The common lifecycle for customers and independent reps.

The next illustration shows the intended effects of training and education on the length of the activity life cycle (in terms of months and years) and on the level of activity (in terms of sales, productivity, frequency, and averages).

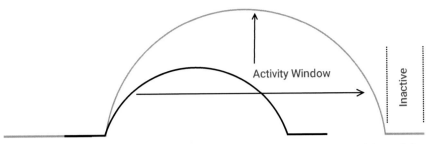

Figure 6–2: Intended effect of training and education, extending the length of the activity period and increasing the level of activity.

- **Structure:** The best training practices suggest a graded structure for training and education that matches phases with intensity of curriculum. Figure 6–3 provides a visual for the five elements, listed below, that make up this graded structure.

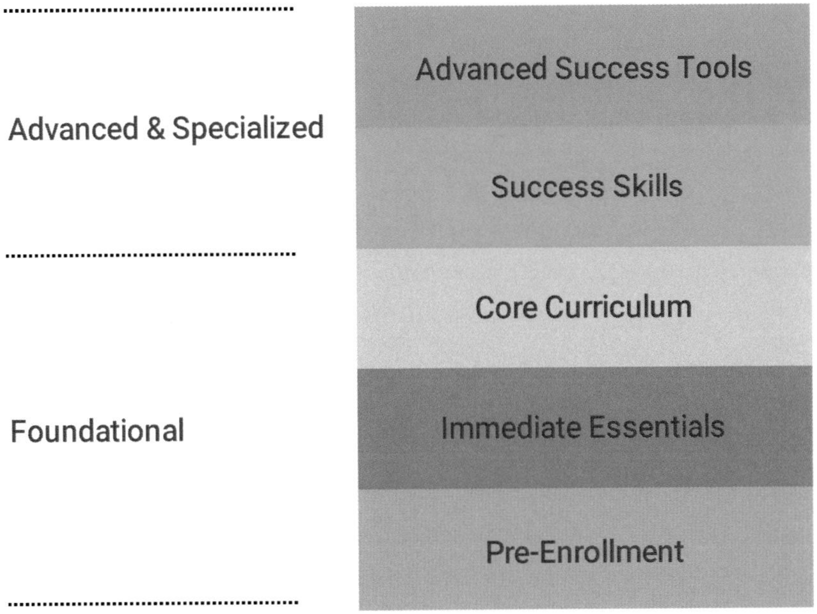

Advanced & Specialized

| Advanced Success Tools |
| Success Skills |
| Core Curriculum |

Foundational

| Immediate Essentials |
| Pre-Enrollment |

Figure 6–3: The Training Triangle.

- ☐ *Pre-Enrollment* must identify the role of the company in accommodating prospects that are exploring the company. This can be done through business presentations, web-based materials, and brochures.

- ☐ *Immediate Essentials* encompasses fast-start training for all new customers and independent representatives, giving them immediate access to training and education that supports their

How to Build a Direct Sales Company　　　　　　　　　　107

decision to become involved with your company, regardless of how involved they intend to be.

- ☐ *Core Curriculum* provides the basic, thorough orientation to products and programs. The core curriculum should be a continuous structured cycle of training modules, permitting serious customers and business builders to jump into the training cycle at any point.

- ☐ *Success Skills* are proven skills and techniques that enhance a business builder's success. These technical skills are associated with crucial communications and business building, drawn from the wide spectrum of skills and tools used by the top builders in your company and around the direct selling industry.

- ☐ *Advanced Success Tools* are high-level tools and skills of leadership and business building.

- **Motivation:** Motivation to participate cannot be assumed; it must be built into the training and education system. This begins with the new customer or independent rep and extends through all phases of development and leadership. The training and education system should work together with recognition, rank advancement, special offerings (products and promotions), and company culture to breed the proper motivation for everyone to participate and grow.

Curriculum Attributes

The most common attributes and features in the best training systems can—and should—guide the evaluation and development of a company's training systems. These attributes and features are outlined below:

- **Best Practices:** Best industry practices must also be applied to a company's training (enrollment processes, customer service systems, internet tools, corporate communications to the field, etc.).

- **Accessible:** Training must be easily accessible by participants.

- **Affordable:** Training must be affordable for participants.

- **Profitable:** Through possible co-development and co-ownership of intellectual property, the education and training program can potentially be a profit center.

- **Effective:** Training must be simple to use and easy to understand, retain, and apply.

In our age of technology, give careful attention to selecting the best media for presentation and training. Each medium has strengths and weaknesses depending on what is being communicated, to whom, and by whom. In evaluating the right medium for the message and the desired result, also keep in mind the importance of balancing cost and return on investment. For examples of the best media platforms to use for specific kinds of training, see Table 6–1 in the Appendix.

Web Training Systems

As we log the weeks, months, and years working with clients, we form opinions and favorites of just about everything. Whether it's a comfort zone or the fact that something simply works, we strive to remain objective, but we don't apologize for aligning with excellent solutions.

When it comes to web training systems for staff and field, we continually seek solutions that work and stay up with the times. For field training, we are particularly keen on systems that allow a company to accomplish the following through a web training system:

- Welcome and orientation for new recruits
- Certification in legally sensitive areas such as product claims
- Basic and advanced training in all aspects of selling, recruiting, and business building
- Management and leadership training
- Motivational and inspirational courses and lessons
- Progressive training that enhances personal development and accountability

ServiceQuest® now offers its own training system, created in partnership with a leading, award-winning technology and virtual training enterprise with two decades and millions of dollars in development to back it. Whether you wish to deliver a quick training to all new recruits that cover your legal bases or if you wish to extend your curriculum farther and faster than you dreamed possible, make your wish list and give ServiceQuest® an opportunity to provide you with a superior training business, helping you every step of the way.

Personal Development

By focusing on an individual's personal development, you can connect with them at a level where you can share values. Genuine interest in the personal development of each individual in your organization, combined with the dedication of resources and energy to help people progress, is a noble end. Nice byproducts are deeper loyalty, greater personal success, and ultimately lasting success for your company.

Personal development takes on a variety of shades, ranging from communication skills that can be used not only in business but also at home, to tax-tracking skills, speaking and presentation skills, memorization skills, and more. We challenge you, as an owner or executive in your direct selling company, to make personal development of all your people a commitment.

The 13-Week Rule

Discussion of a training curriculum for a direct selling company must include the stark reminder that half of all first-year attrition occurs in the first 13 weeks. In other words, if 100 reps join in January and by December only 20 remain (80 percent attrition, or 80 go inactive), half of those 80 will be gone in 13 weeks.

This gives rise to the urgency (and opportunity) to focus start-up training on greater numbers of successful arrivals who make it past the first 13 weeks. Thus, our first rule of training is the 13-week rule: develop training that ensures the success of your fast-start programs.

Company Culture Training

As obscure as it may seem, an important aspect of the training curriculum is to identify and teach (as well as live) the cultural aspects of your company. These vary widely, including training on jargon and terminology, branding elements and how to use them, traditions and rituals, and other elements such as the stories behind the choice of mascots or icons that are shown on pins and certificates.

Give careful thought to the foundation you set for your company's culture, starting with the names and branding signals you create and extending to the training you establish.

A Lesson from Amway

After decades of building and learning, and as a top-ten global direct selling leader, Amway has recognized an important truth. In 2010, Amway commissioned a study that involved ServiceQuest® and TARP (the global customer service research company). The purpose of the study was to quantify their belief that the majority of independent reps, though compensated for recruiting and training, only earned commissions by recruiting.

The results revealed that 17 percent of independent reps included training and development for their recruits and business organizations. Moreover, 62 percent of respondents indicated that they believed the company was responsible for training all who joined, and 19 percent indicated that they felt the responsibility was a shared one. Only six percent indicated that training and recruiting others into the business was their full and complete responsibility as an independent rep.

As a result, Amway has begun the gargantuan process of engineering a training system that helps all new recruits through an orientation and development process in their first 90 days following sign-up. The theory is that once trained in the basics, they will have a greater chance of succeeding. The company has stated that as it steps up to be responsible for all new recruits, those who still receive training from their uplines will benefit even more. The take-away for you as a start-up is that you don't need to wait until you're as big as Amway to provide the training path for your new recruits.

Conclusion

Start today in developing the training and development system your independent reps need. Follow the action steps below to create the tools and systems that will allow you to succeed.

Essential Action Steps for Launching

☐ Develop your independent representative training and development system

☐ Create training videos and tutorials/DVDs

☐ Set up your company's web learning system

☐ Create tools for enhancing rep effectiveness

Launch Smart!

Chapter 7
Operations

Having strong operation systems right at the beginning of your business will help your business grow smoothly and strengthen the relationships you have with those who work with you. There are several core operational systems that you will need to have, so let's get started.

Creating an Extraordinary Experience

On the first day of Terrel's new job at Melaleuca in 1988, CEO Frank VanderSloot met with him to talk about his responsibilities. Frank said, "Your job description is to keep the distributors happy. If you perform as I think you will, you'll naturally build the support structure around you to make sure that happens. So, you're in charge of everything except sales and marketing, and the finance director will also report to me. Otherwise, go and build an enterprise that keeps distributors happy."

Terrel took the charge of keeping the independent reps happy seriously, and he was supported 100 percent in his quest of creating an extraordinary experience for and serving the independent reps. This discovery became the driving passion behind his consulting company, which he created after he left Melaleuca five years later. He called his firm ServiceQuest®.

Probably the simplest and most powerful principle that backs all our teachings in business process development can be found in the model that has been so elegantly perfected by Tony Hsieh, CEO of Zappos. com. This model states that a person's pathway to loyalty at Zappos. com begins with the product experience, which exposes them to the company's customer service systems and people. "Wow!" is their goal. The customer service experience, along with the emotional connections forged along the way, is the gateway to being invited into the company's culture. Hsieh believes that experiencing the Zappos.com culture is what serves as their competitive differentiator and the key to loyalty.

Since 1988, ServiceQuest® has advised direct selling companies in coaching and training to create extraordinary organizations that serve reps with purpose and passion. Clients that have deeply committed themselves to the success of their independent reps have realized that their operations reflect their commitment, passion, and vision and that the right people can bring it all together. The result can be an extraordinary experience for the rep.

Business Processes and Best Practices

Inside the halls of the greatest direct selling companies in the world, the collective successes and failures are linked to the adherence, or lack of adherence, to established business processes, which are designed around the pursuit of best practices.

The core underlying processes are the same. We advocate immediate implementation of these business processes. As your business takes off, you will not have time to change fundamental processes and your growth could quickly overwhelm you. We know because this is usually when our phones ring. Once you implement these processes, they can evolve to accommodate any level of growth.

Don't Prevent Beneficial Change

We can promise you that once you have business processes in place and your company is consistent in adhering to policies that support these processes, you will obtain consistent results. Be sensitive to the risks associated with replacing these principles with your own rules that may go outside the framework we have presented in the ServiceQuest® *Business Process Guide*, a companion book to this start-up guide. There is much to be learned from those who have gone before you.

With that being said, never, never, never allow policies to prevent beneficial change. Encourage innovation and provide clear channels for improving processes in ways that respond to the recommendations and requests from front-line employees, who will always be your best and greatest hope for identifying the bugs that often result from varying away from intended trajectories. Small defects in your processes in the early days of your business will only grow as the company grows.

Instead of looking for people upon whom to heap blame and shame, accept that change will be constant and that great leaders understand and embrace the growth (personal and professional) that comes to all who work together to build a great organization.

Core Operational Competencies

The following nine areas comprise the core operational competencies around which we develop business processes. Because they are thoroughly addressed in the ServiceQuest® *Business Process Guide* we offer here only a brief introduction to show how they apply to the launch process.

Independent Rep Accounts and Enrollment Processing

Enrollment processing provides the critical path for serving all new customers and independent reps. The enrollment process can be a simple system, yet it is the crucial first step in the business process. Failure to master the design and management of this process creates an effect that will ripple through the company, affecting virtually every element of output. An account properly set up can yield astonishing cost savings—costs that otherwise cut into company profits. These costs are due to poor customer service and any costs caused by poor initial decisions.

The goal of our work is to help make the enrollment process a simple, predictable, scalable, and flexible system. This is accomplished through multiple avenues and media, including telephone, internet, mail, and fax. In the ServiceQuest® *Business Process Guide* and through our LaunchSmart coaches, you will be presented standards, processes, illustrations and blueprints, forms, reports, checklists, and model systems and processes to help you launch and improve your enrollment and independent representative and customer account maintenance system.

Order Entry

Order entry and processing is the core of your business. Commissions are wholly dependent on orders. The order process consists of multiple steps, each of which has potential problems and pitfalls. If one of the steps breaks down, the order cannot be successfully completed, disappointing the customer, independent representative, and company.

The objective of your order entry system is to help assure the consistent, accurate, and timely processing and fulfilling of orders. The order process should be a simple, predictable, scannable, and flexible system that is accomplished in a variety of media.

Inventory and Warehouse Management

The independent rep experience is ultimately found in the details. When details are thoughtfully and thoroughly worked out, the entire business experience is smoother and more enjoyable for customers, independent representatives, vendors, staff, and executives.

Every detail has a potential trajectory path that is easily blown out of proportion. If inventory quantities go out of balance, quantity on hand slowly becomes less reliable, backorders appear, orders are not completed, commission volumes are held, qualifications are placed in jeopardy, cash flow is halted on that order, and confidence suddenly trembles. This can cause employees to become more tentative in responses they provide to callers, independent representatives to cross their fingers when they order, and executives to review reports with constant gnawing in the backs of their minds. As inaccuracies breed doubt, minds become cluttered and energy is diverted.

We recommend careful and complete implementation of the warehousing and fulfillment process, including inventory processes. The key functions that relate to inventory processes include the standard postings and their effect on inventory. The ServiceQuest® *Business Process Guide* will take you through the processes of receiving stock, making warehouse transfers, and managing the daily processes in the lifecycle of an order as they pertain to the inventory function.

Order Fulfillment

Picking and packing orders is the vital link between order entry and processing on the front-end of the critical path and the arrival of the package at the doorstep. Accurately picking and verifying orders and shipments is the essence of successful order fulfillment in direct selling companies. Understanding the shipping process rests on accurate account setup, inventory setup and management, and order entry and process. The result is well worth the effort for happy employees and happy reps.

End-of-day Settlement

Daily settlement systems done well make headaches go away. Activities in the daily settlement process assume the following conditions exist in your company's daily operations:

- Independent reps are being entered into the system (by employees and/or by other reps)
- Inventory is established and kept up-to-date
- Orders are being placed and payments are being processed and collected
- Ship verification is consistently updated

Daily transactions are like wet concrete: the ingredients are blended throughout the day in a mixer. These ingredients include independent representative accounts, orders, payments, pick and pack, shipping, and all real-time elements throughout the day. The blend hardens like concrete once it goes through the end-of-day settlement processes, which make transactions permanent.

These daily settlement processes focus on the following essential tasks:

- Pre-settlement processes
- Running settlement
- Post-settlement processes

Settlement primarily consists of depositing cash receipts, updating organizational volumes, and posting transactions to the account credits and accounts receivable ledgers. These steps are automatic when running settlement. The pre-settlement and post-settlement processes require close attention to ensure accurate results.

Before proceeding, the following staff functions must be trained and closely involved with the processes:

- System Administrator (Process Manager and Computer System Administrator)
- Order Entry Manager
- Independent Representative Service Manager
- Warehouse/Shipping Manager

We do recognize the reality of one person taking on several of these responsibilities. We encourage not only a good night's sleep, an indefatigable sense of humor, and a good support network but also a commitment to creating and documenting processes so that someone can easily pick up any of the routine tasks that may become unwieldy for the operations person taking on multiple roles. This quick introduction to the daily settlement process is intended to frame a context and set expectations for proper implementation.

Customer Service

Extraordinary customer service requires extraordinary people and processes to yield extraordinary results. Customer service is arguably at the core of all you do. Reps want to be wealthy, successful, and happy. By being attentive to your relationship with each independent rep and creating emotional connections, you contribute to the rep's success and happiness (this doesn't mean your reps will burst into tears of joy over a smooth customer service experience, but it does happen). Your reps can discover your company's positive culture through good service. With all of this in mind, we maintain that customer service is the new competitive battleground.

Today's reps are more sophisticated than ever before, and they have some amazing options. So, it's not unusual for them to take their business and loyalties elsewhere if they do not receive exceptional support. This includes proactive support, not just when they call you for help.

We observe how commission plans are imitated. We see a parade of valuable and useful products, and we associate with visionary, passionate, and effective corporate leaders. These are no longer the great differentiators. The differentiator is the independent rep experience, particularly in the relationship foundation, emotional connections, and loyalty. This can only occur on a foundation of solid processes and consistent, extraordinary responses and responsiveness from your independent representative service team.

Serving our independent reps is the main focus of our training systems. We emphasize on the elements that comprise successful service experiences supported by the business processes. You can (and should) engineer certain processes to create extraordinary and consistent experiences within your business processes. Processes, technology, and training should all converge and result in great experiences for customers and independent reps. We provide more best practices coaching and training in the ServiceQuest® *Business Process Guide* where we present the real-world aspects of how software, policies, and practice interact with each other.

Accounting

The efforts of everyone within (employees) and without (field organization) your company are posted for display. The measure of success—the scoreboard—is reported by accounting. The accounting function discloses the grade, whether it's a D or an A, to judge how well your company business processes measure up.

Generally, the strength of direct selling software applications will not be found in accounting but in the how they support accounting and business processes. One of the activities to build into your launch plan is the task of integrating the summary information into your choice of accounting system, such as Quickbooks® or PeachTree®.

Administration

The administration function refers to the administration of business processes that has the responsibility to ensure business processes are operating properly. In many organizational charts, *administration* refers to the physical plant, office operations, etc. In our world, we refer to the *System Administrator* as the individual on the lookout for potential problems that can hold up processes such as not posting orders or shipments that have not been ship verified. This function is accountable (as an individual administrator as well as a departmental team) to both company management as well as to the independent rep force who depends on 24/7 effectiveness of the business processes.

The success of a fast-growth, direct selling company is found in its ability to respond to change. Every direct selling organization must build into its very structure the management of change. Examples of change that can plague a fast-growing company are:

- Legally mandated issues such as evolving customer requirements
- Sales-driven challenges that respond to trends and newly discovered sales techniques

- Marketing-based opportunities in an ever-evolving global market based more and more in technology
- Relationship and connection-based situations
- Growth and scale-related demands, including manufacturing, financial, and fulfillment
- Technology-driven mandates

Regardless of the sources and types of change, adaptation and innovation are essential. As circumstances require, system administrators can keep up by understanding their business processes and knowing the settings within their enterprise application. Familiarity with these can alleviate, if not delay, the need for much of the custom programming that is costly and sometimes aggravating.

Commissions

The commission processes are the main attraction for everyone. Thousands of hours of effort culminate in this event, bringing fervor and expectancy from both field organization and company alike. The validity of the compensation plan and its business processes are uncovered for all to see. When the experience is successful and as expected, confidence peaks. When it's not, the clock begins a fast countdown to disappointment and suspicion.

When home office staff view themselves as a team, and when accountability is expected from department heads, problems are taken care of. When everybody realizes that they play a role in assuring accurate commissions, management magic happens. Once the main event arrives and obstacles are handled upstream, the burden of the system administrator's job is lightened. We preach cooperation and unity with the successful commission experience as your target. It's the main part in having happy reps.

To set the stage for commission processing and checklists, we first make the case for consistency in processes. The commission process begins the moment a new account, order, or credit card is entered or whenever adjustments are made. The accuracy of a commission run is placed into jeopardy whenever anybody places an order on hold or makes adjustments without understanding all of the implications (thus the importance of selecting and training the right people and then trusting them and holding them accountable). This becomes more likely since dozens of people encounter the accounts and orders as they navigated through the system.

Accurate commissions truly are the responsibility of every employee. In the grander scheme, the company has three promises to keep, and all employees are engaged in this quest:

- Product promise (quality product delivered on time)
- Commission promise (accurate commissions paid on time)
- Service promise (caring, competent, consistent service whenever needed)

Conclusion

The way you run the operations of your business will determine your independent representative, customer, and staff's happiness. When your people are happy, your business will run more smoothly. Follow the action steps below to put your business operations together.

Essential Action Steps for Launching

- ☐ Select office and warehouse location
- ☐ Organize your team and create your staffing plan
- ☐ Design your staff selection and development plan
- ☐ Source your products
- ☐ Create and set up your distribution and fulfillment system
- ☐ Identify suppliers and secure terms and relationships

Chapter 8
Staff

One of the most helpful staffing tips Terrel ever received came early in his career from his billionaire boss: "We don't train people to be nice; we hire nice people." With this bit of advice, Terrel's boss handed him the job of expanding the service operation of the fast-growing company. The guidelines and practices in this section will give you a great deal of practical help and confidence in creating a team of people who will take good care of your sales organization.

Staff Planning

The objective in staffing is to support your independent reps and help them to be highly successful by creating a high standard of service and responsiveness in the support center. Key variables in your staffing plan will include the level of technology you use, the cross-training and skill sets of your staff, your attitude toward constant improvement and root-cause analysis, your product mix, the use of party plan (retail) or network marketing (consumption), and other variables that work together to create the dynamics of who calls and how often.

When making and executing the staffing plan, consider the importance of hiring staff who come with a variety of skill sets. These staff members can address a breadth of demands by holding multiple rolls, and they can go deeper and not as wide when the company grows. This is especially ideal at the early stages of operations when resources are scarce.

Staffing Recommendations

If you have a resource budget that just meets your minimum requirements, you will need to have a "bare-bones," or minimum, staffing team. Below is a list of positions we recommend you will need at the prelaunch of your business as well as our suggestion for how soon to hire them and what to expect from them:

- Customer Service Manager
  - ☐ Hire as early as possible
  - ☐ Must learn how the company works by helping to set it up (compensation design, fulfillment, software selection, etc.)
- Customer Service Rep
  - ☐ Hire six weeks prior
  - ☐ Specifically select for maturity, skill sets, and multitasking abilities
  - ☐ Over-hire and expect fast advancement
- General Manager/CEO
  - ☐ Provides vision and leadership
  - ☐ A servant leader over marketing (product development, etc.)
- Tech-head
  - ☐ Hire early
  - ☐ Involved in compensation plan design, site selection, technology specifications, hardware, network, office applications, phone system, etc.
- Executive Assistant
  - ☐ Supports the general and customer service managers
  - ☐ Performs all executive support functions, handles basic bookkeeping functions, and takes independent representative service calls
  - ☐ Highly organized and creates order out of the chaos that will surround start-up
- Fulfillment Team
  - ☐ Insures that orders are fulfilled and services are delivered
  - ☐ Fulfills the commitments made by the company when costumers and independent reps initiate product sales
  - ☐ Can be in-house or third-party
- Sales Executive
  - ☐ Focuses on field development

Once you have launched you will need a more moderate sized team, so you will need to add additional staffing roles. These are our recommendations for the additional staffing rolls you will need post-launch:

- Customer Service Reps (additional to the ones hired prelaunch)
  - ☐ Starts by handling emails and plans to evolve to phones
- Design/Marketing Support
  - ☐ Handles website maintenance, updates, communications, newsletter, etc.
- Expanded IT
  - ☐ Supports operations

To see the results of a study that illustrates the staff resource efficiencies (how much revenue the company can produce for each employee on the payroll), see Table 8–1 of the Appendix.

Common Staffing Rolls

These are the most common staffing roles that a company must fill early on:

- Finance and Accounting
- Technology
- Marketing
- Fulfillment
- Administration
- Human Resources
- Sales Support
- Legal and Compliance
- Executive Staffing and Support

Rep Service Representatives

Rep Service Representatives (RSA) are the company employees that provide customer and independent rep support. There are several RSA roles. Below are a list of these roles and the minimum requirements that each should have:

- Director (Rep Service Director)
  - ☐ Five years of customer service management experience
  - ☐ Call center experience is helpful but not required
  - ☐ Bachelor's degree, Master's degree (MA, MS, MBA, MAcc), four to ten years of related business experience and/or training, or equivalent combination of education and experience
  - ☐ Demonstrated interpersonal skills (warmth, caring, competence)
- Assistant (Rep Service Specialist)
  - ☐ Three years of call center experience
  - ☐ One year of call traffic management and scheduling
- Supervisor (Rep Service Supervisor)
  - ☐ Two years of supervisory experience over seven or more people
  - ☐ Two years of call center experience
  - ☐ High school diploma
  - ☐ Demonstrated telephone skills (warmth, care, competence)
- Representative (Level II or Rep Service Representative)
  - ☐ High school diploma
  - ☐ Demonstrated telephone skills (warmth, care, competence)
- Specialist (Level III or Rep Service Specialist)
  - ☐ High school diploma
  - ☐ One year of college/university/technology schooling
  - ☐ Demonstrated telephone skills (warmth, care, competence)

The People in Customer Service

In our world, everybody is a customer service agent. Some have special assignments to work in accounting, marketing, and so forth. The common profile of the people who work in the best customer service centers is "hearts and smarts," as seen below:

- Hearts that care
- Empathy—They feel what the caller feels and demonstrate that they feel it

- Affirm—They validate the person. No problem is too big or too small; if it's important to the caller, it's important to us
- Initiative—They take charge; they are good at what they do
- Smarts
- Competent—They know the company, products, compensation, computers, how things work, and how to get things fixed
- They can analyze and apply abstract concepts to come up with concrete results
- They have basic mathematical and analytical skills (this is often shown through grades they earned in math and algebra and through computer skills, interests, etc.)

Staffing Variables

In considering how to staff the start-up, there are several variables that will determine how much customer service help you will need and how many customer service reps to hire.

Customer Support

A network marketing company typically requires more customer service staff than a party plan company. This difference is important to consider when planning the staffing needed for your company:

- **Network marketing—Consumption Model:** Customers buy and independent reps sign on directly with the company. Because of this, their customer service issues are more commonly handled directly with the company. This results in a heavier reliance on the company, which, in turn, causes an increase in calls and a heavier load.

- **Party Plan—Retail Model:** Independent reps develop their own business as they go out and find hosts for their parties. Because of this, they handle many of the customer service issues while they work with their host. In a sense, the business has built-in customer service through the independent rep. This results in a heavier reliance on reps for customer service, and, in turn, reps rely on their upline and company for support. This causes a decrease in calls and a lighter load on the company.

Technology

Whether you have high- or low-tech will be an important variable to consider. Below are some reasons why:

- High-tech (automated help desk, knowledge base, etc.):
  - ☐ More dependence on technology-related support
  - ☐ Less dependence on basic support, such as order entry and enrollment
  - ☐ Higher dependence on high-level business support, which results in fewer calls and lighter load. The trade-off is that there is generally a higher attrition trend
- High-touch (low-tech):
  - ☐ Less dependence on technology-related support
  - ☐ More dependence on basic support since information is not readily available, such as order entry and enrollment
  - ☐ Standard/normal dependence on high-level business support resulting in potentially higher calls and heavier load. The trade-off is that there is generally a lower attrition trend

Cross-training and Skill Sets

The level of cross-training and skill sets customer service staff have will also affect your staffing needs:

- High Level of Cross-training and Skill Sets:
  - ☐ Fewer calls
  - ☐ Shorter call handle time (and thus, greater return on staff investment)
  - ☐ Creates efficiencies, reducing the number of staff required
- More calls when compartmentalized groups (basic vs advanced)
  - ☐ Basic: orders, enrollments, information
  - ☐ Advanced: business support, commissions, policy administration, advanced problems related to orders and enrollments

Crisis Management

Your company's ability to manage crisis is a variable that should not be overlooked:

- Crisis Management
  - ☐ Whether small or gargantuan, the key is to be prepared
  - ☐ Fast response and planned communications that reassure the company's values, training opportunities, and access to information are the keys
  - ☐ Better crisis management equals lighter impact on support center, overall small ratios of staff to field

One-call Resolution

Another variable to consider is your ability to have one-call resolution (when a caller can receive help from the first person they talk to and does not need to be passed onto someone else). Here are some points to think about when creating one-call resolution:

- Access to information required to research (one-touch research) and resolve
  - ☐ Better access equals higher percentage of one-call resolution
  - ☐ Limited access equals lower percentage of one-call resolution
- Authority and training
  - ☐ More authority results in a higher percentage of one-call resolution
  - ☐ Less authority results in a lower percentage of one-call resolution
- Accountability and feedback
- Awaiting approvals, information, and actions from internal third-party

Communication

With all of these variables previously mentioned, effective communication is one of upmost importance. Consider how highly effective communication will benefit your independent reps over less effective communication:

- Highly effective communication:
  - ☐ Yields happier reps and happier staff

- [ ] Increased sense of being a valued "insider"
- [ ] Faster and more effective deployment/acceptance of initiatives and information sent out
- [ ] Staff learns from company instead of finding out from field
- [ ] Fewer calls
- [ ] Fewer customer service staff required
- Less effective communication:
  - [ ] Puts greater volume and pressure on independent rep support operation

Service Leadership

Overall, it is through the foundation of servant leadership that the rest of the considerations hold up. *Service leadership* is when the leadership is focused on serving those who work under them. It is the foundation for creating a team of service professionals who are highly capable of performing. All the team really needs is an executive champion that serves them and helps them succeed.

Interview Methodology

In general, we have always found that it is best to hire for attitude and train for skills. The question is, "How do you hire for attitude?" The best way is to put the interviewee into a situation they might encounter at work and see how they handle it. For a call center hire, this might mean seeing how they answer the phone.

There are five key questions you should ask yourself about the candidate, especially when hiring in a fast-growth company:

- Can the person do this job?
- Can they do it in this environment?
- Can they do the job on an ongoing basis?
- Can they solve problems?
- Can they recognize their own failures?

Ask your interviewees for specific examples of problem solving skills they have used in other situations (work environment or not). Ask about previous successes and failures to gauge if they are willing to learn from their mistakes.

Example: Interview

The goal of the interview is to discover whether this person will be an excellent independent representative of a culture of care and competence by learning who they really are. Your tactic must be to "get real" so you can get to know the person. Drill deep into the conversation to discover how candidates thinks, what their underlying values are, what their maturity level is, and how they would fit into your company's culture.

You: Tell me about your boss at the Gas-n-Go.

Candidate: Well, she was fair, and she expected us to be on time.

You: What do you mean by 'she was fair'?

Candidate: She didn't have favorites and expected everybody to pull their own weight.

You: What would you do if you ever felt that a manager was showing favorites, and it wasn't you?

This example illustrates how you can use a candidate's resume/application as a springboard to get to know him or her. The interviewer was relaxed and followed her instinct as she let the conversation go where it should go.

Questions and Topics to Always Avoid

There are certain questions you should never ask and topics you should always avoid when interviewing a candidate. Below is a list of these kind of questions and topics:

- Race or color
- Religion

- National origin
- Sex
- Sexual preference
- Marital status or spouse's employment
- Age
- Disability—You may ask if there is a disability that would interfere with ability to perform the job for which they have applied, but you can't ask, "Do you have a disability?" or "Have you ever been treated for any diseases?"
- Names—Specifically don't ask if they have changed their name or if they have ever worked under a different name
- Duration of residence at current address
- Birthplace
- Photograph
- Citizenship
- Languages—You may ask if they speak, read, or write a foreign language, but you can't ask where or how they acquired the ability to speak, read, or write it
- Character—You may not ask questions such as "Have you ever been arrested?"
- Relatives—You can't ask for names, addresses, ages, or other information concerning an applicant's children or other relatives that are not employed by the company
- Organizations—You may ask if they are a member of any clubs, societies, lodges, etc., but you can't ask them to list the places they are members of

Questions You Can Ask

There are many questions that you can ask in an interview. These are the top three kinds of questions you should ask and examples of good questions within these categories:

- **Open-ended Questions:** Avoid questions that can be answered "yes" or "no," but be specific. ("Tell me about yourself" is probably too open ended, though it could be a good question to determine maturity.)

- [ ] Why have you chosen this field?
- [ ] How much do you know about our company? About network marketing and direct selling?
- [ ] What are your strengths, and how do they relate to our company?
- [ ] Tell me about your last job?
- [ ] If I were to contact your previous employer(s), with your permission, what would he or she likely say about your work performance?
- [ ] What is important to you in a job?
- [ ] Is there anything you would like to tell me, or add to any of your previous answers?

- **Probes:** This type of question allows the applicant to do the talking while you can observe to clarify facts and attitudes.

- [ ] Do you enjoy talking to people on the telephone?
- [ ] Why are you leaving your present position?
- [ ] How well do you take criticism? What is your attitude about feedback?
- [ ] Is working under pressure a problem?
- [ ] Do you think you could represent a product you do not believe in? How would you go about establishing your belief in our products?
- [ ] Describe a personality conflict you have had with a coworker. How did you deal with it and how did it affect your job?
- [ ] What system do you have for checking your own work?
- [ ] Would you object to dress and grooming standards?
- [ ] This job reports directly to me; what would you look for in a working relationship with me?
- [ ] How would you feel if your supervisor asked you to do an additional task not in your job description?
- [ ] How do you define success?

- **Closed-ended Questions:** Sometimes it is good to add a few of these. If a candidate avoids the question, or you cannot pin down a response, it may be an indication that the candidate wants to evade a particular area, and it should be explored in more depth.

  ☐ Are you able to work overtime when necessary?

  ☐ What are your thoughts on working additional hours, last minute, weekends, or holiday if needed? Our shifts will include Saturdays; will that be a problem?

  ☐ Can you accommodate changes to your shift?

  ☐ Do you consider your commute too long or too tiring?

  ☐ Have you ever punched a time clock before?

  ☐ Do you consider keeping up-to-date on developments in your field through outside reading as part of the job?

Conclusion

People truly are your greatest assets, and direct selling is fundamentally a people business. Understanding this gives you nearly everything you need; the rest can be filled in. Below are the action steps to take to establish a strong staff.

Essential Action Steps for Launching

☐ Develop your Staffing Plan

☐ Organize and launch your Independent Representative Service Strategy

☐ Set the cultural tone for the home office

☐ Hire nice people

Chapter 9
Software & Technology

Some owners and CEOs will tell you that the biggest challenge they face in direct selling is the feeling of no control over their technology. The tradeoff today for most popular web-based applications is easy access and relatively low-cost entry in exchange for control over data mining and customization. At first this is troublesome, and as your company grows, this tradeoff causes even more difficulties.

Despite this, start-ups often conclude that they will give the low-cost, easy-entry option a whirl and upgrade if and when the need arises. As consultants, this line of thinking is by far the most challenging for us to change. It is always better to start out right instead of later on having to fix problems that could have been avoided.

The Challenge

If you are launching a new network marketing or party plan company, the challenge you will face is choosing the right technology foundation to invest in. Your independent reps will average fewer than 10 working hours per week, so it is imperative your software solution is flexible, nimble, and simple to use. Your staff will be small with shared resources, so they need easy-to-use reports, screens, and information. Given the financial strains on a new business, getting the right technology solution and understanding the investment needed is an essential ingredient in the start-up success formula.

The objective in technology specialization is to help your company and reps become highly successful by leveraging the best technological tools and services that match your company's unique needs. You will need a:

- Solid technology platform and scalable plan in place at launch
- Software provider or in-house team selected, prepared, and excited to serve

- Technology implementation plan that meets launch objectives
- Disaster recovery plan that anticipates all possible contingencies

Software to Meet Growing Needs

The emerging phase is one of the most exciting, rewarding, and challenging stages. At this stage of company growth, you may feel like you are really hitting your stride, increasing revenues, and adding many new independent reps and bottom line profits. At the same time, the demands on you and your staff grow as your sales force does.

Statistics show on average that direct selling companies annually lose 70 to 80 percent of their sales force. Lack of clear, concise, and efficient communication creates frustration among your sales force. This then causes retention to suffer. At a minimum, accurate order processing and on-time shipping, combined with accurate and timely commission and bonus payments, are vital to your success. You will also desire to have greater control of key business functions, so you are not as reliant on third parties who may inhibit your growth. Companies are often frustrated when their software partners cannot respond in a cost-effective and timely manner.

Recruiting customers, hosts, and new reps is essential to growing a network marketing or party plan business. As groups of customers and independent representatives expand, it is not unusual for a genealogy or downline to consist of thousands, even hundreds of thousands, extending many levels and generations deep. Along the way, some of the most complex business processes you will need to integrate include ordering, fulfillment, commissions, returns, sponsoring, promotions, ranks, inventory, sales tax, and web services.

Seek technology solutions that allow you to add in functionality as required. What you may require at 20,000 independent reps will be vastly different than what you require at 1,000 reps or 150,000 reps. Consider some of the tools for expansion:

- Managing compensation plans easily
- Creating, managing, and tracking incentive programs
- Streamlined administrative functions with events and actions functionality
- Maintaining consistent communications and branding

- Analytics for a clear understanding of your business
- Integrated online sales force management tools

Successful companies do not continue to grow and offer a continued competitive edge without being efficient, which is often vital as multiple technology platforms come into play. If your business model calls for manufacturing, then at the right point, you should consider Manufacturing Requirements Planning; in all cases, growth demands Enterprise Requirements Planning (EPR). If the approach is to customize an ERP solution, it can be one of the most difficult and costly undertakings, which often results in substandard solutions. Simply ask around and you will see what we mean.

As you become established, you will want greater control and business management tools that you can use in-house. You will be looking for competitive tools that can be utilized to continually motivate the sales force as they grow, resulting in your company's growth. Some of the solutions you will need include:

- In-house business management tools that offer greater control, flexibility, and application tailoring with less reliance on third-party software providers
- Compensation plan "what if" capabilities for assessing various recruiting, retention, and sales behaviors
- Robust reporting on all key sales performance indicators. This includes recruiting, sales, retention, and incentives at all company levels (executive, mid-management and sales force), and provides the opportunity to see which programs are working the best, to discover sales force high-achievers, etc.
- Global expansion options in a streamlined system that anyone in your company can easily access and understand worldwide
- Innovative sales performance analytics to help make better business decisions

Technology Strategy

Technology in this era of business provides a wide array of options, but there are solid conventions and foundations that you can build on. Consider these principles that should drive your technology strategy:

- Clear requirements to guide the technology strategy
- Streamlined software implementation on-time and within budget
- Software that can be used like a utility; pay as you grow
- Flexibility in the definition of your compensation and incentive plans
- Early control of your brand
- Built-in communication tools for your sales force
- Online sales force tools that will make you look like a bigger, sophisticated, and established company to make it easier to attract new recruits into your business
- Assistance from our professional services team to help you provide additional incentive programs, reports, and more

Software and Operations

The vehicle for transporting your company's strategic plan into reality is software and operations. The success formula of the ages is Vision + Passion + Action = Success. The surest way to action is to use the right network marketing software and to implement sound operations. The best operation practices assure efficiency, productivity, speed, and accuracy.

Generating recurring income is the most straightforward and well-understood management imperative of business operations. Decades of research and in-the-trenches work with direct selling companies have shaped the development matrix that guides the establishment of goals, design, management, and competencies at three levels of operations: the organization level, process level, and performance level.

Designed to help entrepreneurial and early-stage companies, the LaunchSmart™ system framework assists owners and executives to see into the future and to design the company on a foundation that will hold up under the strain of growth. Emphasizing best practices and proven competencies, the approach is to create a scalable operation that relies on processes and systems that are created and managed by people who wish to grow with the company.

As a result of 20 years in and around direct selling and party plan software, we remain convinced that there is no perfect software solution. We keep a report card of many of the software providers to keep note of our favorites and the scoundrels. We see our role as helping to shape and influence the design and delivery of network marketing and party plan technology solutions.

Build or Buy?

From our viewpoint, the single greatest risk that a company faces when deciding to build (design their own software) or buy (purchase software from a vendor who is designing it as they go) is that new developers typically do not understand the challenges involved. They either come from a traditional business environment and understand business rules and operations, or they come from the unique world of network marketing genealogies, party plan commissions, and host incentives but fall considerably short in their knowledge of business rules and best practices. Either way, the result can be catastrophic.

We hold the opinion that the direct selling profession is so small when compared to more standard business enterprises that it does not yet compete for the attention of the full-featured business enterprise software developers. This is not to say that we are critical of the talented and devoted developers and programmers who serve the direct selling profession; it's to say that the network marketing and party plan software solutions as a whole are at the front-end of their maturity curves. There is still a lot of work to do to get it right.

Thus, whether you create your own software or whether you purchase an existing solution and adapt it to your business needs, you must be prepared to be involved, smart, and patient.

Build or Buy Considerations

We have organized three questions to consider when asking, "Should I build or buy?" These apply to your team as well as to developers and programmers of a pre-built network marketing or party plan system:

- How experienced are the members of the software development team in the following components of network marketing/direct sales software?

  ☐ Order management

- [ ] Customer/independent representative service management
- [ ] Call center demands
- [ ] Computer-telephone integration
- [ ] Customer relationship management
- [ ] Payment processing
- [ ] Commission processing
- [ ] Genealogy maintenance
- [ ] Returns and exchanges
- [ ] Accounting
- [ ] Inventory
- [ ] Shipping and fulfillment
- [ ] Adjustments
- [ ] Administration

- What are the true costs of development? Don't underestimate the project's true costs and time to market. Three software companies surveyed provided the following information on developing their software:

Software Company	Man Hours	Development Cost
A	95,000	$3.5 million
B	80,000	$4 million
C	74,880	$2.7 million

What are other key points to consider? Development of in-house projects has a high degree of complexity for a number of reasons that include:

- Required business functionality depth
- Limited inter-operability features of software applications
- Limited in-house development expertise

- Long-term software version upgrading and robust integration/application testing

In a typical in-house development project, the company will have costs in three specific areas:

- **Personnel Costs:** For most companies, this will represent either new development resources or a reassignment of existing resources from other responsibilities. In order to ensure long-term skillset protection, the company should allocate more than one developer. The accumulated personnel cost (salary, benefits, administrative overhead, etc.) over a five-year timeframe for two highly skilled and marketable development resources is approximately $1.8 million or $360,000 a year for four developers.

- **Technical Training:** In order to complete and provide quality software both accurately and in a timely manner, the assigned developers will need specific technical training in the language and tools used to develop and maintain the software. In addition, the company will require the same training as it releases and adopts new software versions. Assuming that each person needs a quarter of a year's worth of training each year, the accumulated training costs over a five-year timeframe for four developers would be approximately $229,000.

- **Hardware Environments:** Establishing an independent development and testing hardware environment that mirrors the company's production environment is critical to successful quality assurance. A company's success with application development and implementation depends on product quality assurance. And in order to realize continued and expanding benefits, the company will need to deploy new versions of the application software as it becomes available. This critical testing environment will require additional hardware/software expenditures. Estimating monthly leases of $5,000, the accumulated five-year expense totals $300,000.

One thing is certain—technology is at the heart of success in direct selling. The direct selling model (network marketing, party plan, and hybrid plans), as a general rule, becomes a more complex model than most traditional business models. It demands all of the functionality of traditional business (selling, fulfillment, customer service, reporting)

and adds the core elements of commissioning and genealogy maintenance, lead management, recognition, and advancements. Whether you
decide to build or buy, stay close to the process, ask a lot of questions,
and resist the temptation to buy an "off-the-shelf" product. So far, we
haven't found a ready-made product that meets the unique needs of
any business without substantial adaptation.

Overall, remember to always start with the fundamentals. Network
marketing and party plan software rely on competent systems and
sub-systems that handle enrollment processing, payment processing,
order processing, returns and exchanges, commission processing, and
customer service administration.

Technology Requirements

Technology supports your business and makes it functional. To understand the need for technology, we will first provide a summary of
a network marketing company and how different factors interconnect
and affect the whole.

Every network marketing company provides a business opportunity to
independent reps. They join for a reasonable fee (usually under $200)
and receive the right to purchase products from their host company
at wholesale prices. When they sell these products to their customers,
they keep the profit (the difference between their wholesale price and
the selling price). In the United States, the Direct Selling Association,
the leading trade group for this type of business, reports that in 2017,
annual sales were $36 billion sold by 21 million independent represen-
tatives.

Recruiting new reps is essential for the growth of the business. Recruiting is done by independent reps seeking to build a downline
organization of other reps selling various products who, in turn, recruit
others into the business. As an independent rep recruits a new rep, he
builds his downline organization person-by-person. His recruits then
do the same, causing his downline organization to grow and his sales
volume to increase which he will receive a small commission for each
month.

In such a manner, a downline organization can grow exponentially
with an ever-increasing number of people seeking others to recruit

under them to sell the company's products to new customers. In some cases, a downline genealogy may number in the thousands and extend many levels deep. Levels are represented by one person sponsoring another. For example, an independent rep who sponsors five other reps has five people on his first level. If each of those five in turn sponsor two others, then the original rep will have ten reps on his second level.

Commissions are paid to the rep from sales that occur within his downline genealogy. A commission will then be profited from personal sales. Every company uses different rules that are designed to promote successful behaviors of the sales force. This set of rules is called the compensation plan. Every network marketing company competes with other network marketing companies based not only on the strength of their products, but also on the strength of their compensation plan. Indeed, a primary factor in the decision of a prospective rep to join any one company is how generous their compensation plan appears to be. A company with a poor compensation plan will find great difficulty attracting new reps to sell its products, while another company with a very enticing compensation plan may grow dramatically as a result.

As you can see from this summary, the factors within network marketing company build upon each other. Technology makes it possible to keep everything running as anticipated. Below we will go into further depth of why proper software is needed for you to avoid problems that can come with genealogy, compensation plans, order processing and refunds, and web access.

Genealogy Management

The compensation plan uses the genealogy relationships to determine:

- Who receives commissions on any particular sale
- How much each individual in the upline (the sponsors above the rep making the sale) receives as a percentage of the sale
- What to do in the event an upline rep does not meet his minimum performance quota

If there are any errors in the genealogy linkages that reflect these sponsor relationships between independent reps, the commissions will be incorrect, and the sales force will lose trust in the company. This is where the use of technology comes in. Any changes made must be updated within your system. If it isn't, these problems can occur which can result in the company having great difficulty recruiting. Independent reps will not bring new people into the business unless they trust the company will take good care of them. Many independent reps will look for other opportunities and leave. The reps remain only if they want to continue working the business. Hence, the accuracy of the genealogy relationships is of paramount importance to the success of a network marketing company.

This downline genealogy imposes unique and challenging tasks on the host company who is charged with managing the many thousands of relationships with perfect accuracy. These relationships or linkages that reflect "who sponsored who" are subject to many changes that must be performed over time. These include:

- **Sponsor Changes:** If an independent rep is entered into the computer system using an incorrect sponsor (Fred Jones instead of Fred James, for example), this relationship must be corrected. Occasionally, a rep will have a falling out with his sponsor and request a sponsor change. Sometimes a company will allow such changes to occur. Any change to the sponsor of a rep requires the computer to not only change the sponsor reference in the rep's record, but also to change the sponsor's list of recruits. The linkage works upward from the rep to the sponsor, and downward from the sponsor to the rep. This bidirectional linkage must be kept intact with perfect precision or commissions will be incorrect.

- **Termination:** When an independent rep resigns or is deemed inactive by the company, they must be removed from the genealogy. The process of removal requires the software to realign all linkages so that there are no holes in the genealogy. If Fred sponsors Bob who sponsors Sally and Joyce, when Bob is terminated, Sally and Joyce must be reassigned to Fred. Again, the bidirectional linkages must be correctly updated.

- **Reinstatement:** Though an independent rep may be terminated for various reasons, some will request to be reinstated. When reinstated, a rep may be restored to his original condition including his rank or title, under his original sponsor (or maybe under a different sponsor), and to his original downline (or not, depending on the company's policies). The software must manage this process with perfect precision and record all changes.

- **Combining Two Distributorships:** In some cases, an independent rep may be entered into the computer multiple times and have new recruits placed under each distributorship. In such cases, these two distributorships must be combined into one. A marriage may also require two independent reps to be combined into one.

Other functionality needed for managing a genealogy include:

- All changes to genealogy linkages must be logged by date and time so customer service staff can respond to inquiries and challenges to changing downline relationships.

- Terminated reps must never be removed from the database in anticipation of the possibility of reinstatement, yet a terminated rep cannot appear on the genealogy, nor be considered in the commission calculations. Their earnings history is also required for tax auditing.

- Unlimited width must be allowed so that an independent rep can sponsor one or thousands of people into his genealogy.

- Unlimited depth must be reported so that the company or a rep with a very large downline genealogy can see the full organization with all of the linkages of sponsorship correctly represented. This report capability is essential for a leader to manage his large organization.

Commissions and Personal Sales

As noted previously, every network marketing company has a compensation plan that embodies a unique set of rules and policies that are used to calculate commissions paid to the sales force. This is based upon the sales that occur within each of their individual downline genealogies. Most compensation plans measure the performance of each independent representative based on:

- Sales within their downline group
- Number of personal recruits
- Achievement level of personal recruits
- Personal sales amounts of their recruits and others below them
- Other performance measurements unique to the company

Based on the individual performance of each rep, the computer software must calculate a commission to pay various reps on every sale. This is paid through the upline genealogy linkages. For example, if Bob sponsors Dan and Dan sponsors Sally, then Dan and Bob are the upline of Sally.

Many reps will have an upline of ten or more people, and the computer must follow the upline person by person, paying each a small commission on the sale by the original rep (Sally in the last example). Hence, a single forty-dollar sale to a customer may involve paying ten or more different people in the upline a different commission amount according to their individual level of achievement and current performance. The formulas involved are complex due to the different levels of performance of each upline rep as well as the complexities of the rules involved. Because of this, your system needs to have the ability to do:

- **Continual Updating:** The commission calculation process cannot interfere with ongoing business. A company cannot, for example, shut down order processing because commissions are calculating. With web technology, each company must offer a 24-hour order entry web page and cannot allow any internal process, such as commission calculation, to interfere with the ongoing business.

- **Commission Statement Reports:** These must be prepared for each independent representative showing them how their commissions were calculated to eliminate most questions or concerns. Considering that some reps may be paid on hundreds, if not thousands of sales in their downline genealogy, this commission statement may be quite involved for some.

- **Exemption System:** Managing thousands of independent representatives brings to the surface many unusual circumstances that must be accommodated in the commission system. When a human error occurs that affects the commissions of a rep, in some cases it is necessary to exempt the rep from specific performance requirements for the current commission month, or even longer. For example, due to an internal human error, a rep might need to be exempted from meeting a monthly hundred-dollar personal sales requirement in order to receive commissions (a rule that is very common). This exemption system allows these exceptions to be done by corporate staff to maintain the integrity and trustworthiness of the company when the company is at fault in an error that affects the rep.

- **Overpayments:** For orders placed by a rep and paid for by check, they must be refunded any overpayment to the purchasing rep through the commission system. These amounts are too small to justify creating a separate check.

- **Underpayments:** Similarly, to overpayments, when a customer gives the independent rep a check for too little, the lost value must be collected from the rep's commission earnings automatically.

- **Balance Forwarding:** Most companies set a minimum check amount (ten dollars is common) before they will issue a commission check to an independent rep. This eliminates the cost of sending out hundreds of checks for nominal amounts. These earnings, however, cannot be erased. Instead, they are carried forward from month to month until finally a rep exceeds the minimum check threshold and receives their earnings.

- **Commission Adjustment System:** When errors or breaches of the company's policies occur, it is customary to adjust future commissions to "make right" the error or breach of policy. For example, an independent rep may purchase a large amount of product and thereby qualifies for a higher commission percentage, but then later return the product for a refund with an intent to defraud the company. Then the original commissions earned by him and his many upline sponsors may be adjusted downward to reflect what they should have earned had he not purchased the large amount of product. Every network marketing company finds a need to process adjustments to commissions that will be reflected on the next commission check. Audit trailing of each adjustment is required. Adjustments must be reported on the independent representative commission statement.

- **Automatic Advancements and Demotions:** According to the compensation plan, advancements and demotions must be done by the software. Most compensation plans include a "career path," or series of titles or ranks of achievement. As an independent representative achieves the next rank or title, their commissions are increased in some fashion. Achievement of a higher rank always involves an increase of performance by the independent rep and his downline. With thousands of reps moving up the career path each month, the software must compute the precise achievement rank for each person before it can determine the formulas to use in computing the person's commission amount. Similarly, demotions in rank are necessary so that an independent rep who fails to maintain their level of performance is not unjustly rewarded. All of these advancements and demotions must be done flawlessly on thousands of reps in the company's downline genealogy according to the precise rules of the compensation plan.

- **Audit Trails of All Commission Calculations:** These are required so the company can validate the accuracy of the software's computations. The company's integrity is at risk when a commission check is sent to an independent representative. If the rep finds errors in the computations, the rep will often resign and seek another company worthier of his or her trust. Hence, every network marketing company requires a mechanism to audit and validate the accuracy of each independent rep's commission calculations.

- **Rerun Capability:** When commissions are calculated and audited, it is common that the first trial run will bring to light errors or suspicious problems to investigate. Inevitably, some issues will require human correction or intervention (such as an exemption for a rep), and then a rerun of the commissions will be necessary. Many companies, in fact, find the need to run commissions several times each month before they can finally approve it. Once the commission calculations are validated, then checks and statements are prepared and sent.

- **Qualifying and Commissionable Volumes:** Most products purchased by independent reps will have commissions paid on the wholesale price paid by the rep. Some products, however, have unique rules associated with their commissionable values. When a product is unusually costly to the company, the company may not be able to afford full commission payments on that product. In such cases, the company may elect to assign a lower basis for commissions called the commissionable value. Commissions are then paid on the commissionable value rather than the wholesale price, thus reducing the cost of commissions for that specific product.

Similarly, the same product may have another value called qualifying volume (often expressed in points) which is used to add to the sales quota required of the purchasing rep (and potentially his upline) instead of the commissionable value. Thus, if a rep bought a widget for twenty dollars wholesale, commissions might be paid on the commissionable value of fifteen dollars and the qualifying volume might be fifty points. This is especially common with international companies. This may add significantly to the complexity of managing the commission system but is required when product margins vary widely on some products offered for sale.

Incentives

Having worked with hundreds of network marketing companies, we are not aware of any companies of reasonable size that have not had special incentive programs to stimulate sales or recruiting in some fashion. Incentive programs work in harmony with the compensation plan to encourage a desired independent representative behavior. Reps who meet the requirements of the incentive are rewarded with prizes, trips, special recognition, or some non-cash reward.

For example, if an independent rep were to sponsor twelve new recruits in a specific six-month time frame, each of whom sells over $1,000, then the rep might earn a free vacation cruise with other reps who did the same. The incentive programs change frequently in each company to keep the sales force enthused about new opportunities. Otherwise, an incentive loses its excitement and power to motivate the participating reps.

As an integral part of the strategy to motivate the sales force, an incentives system is required to manage the complex criteria and performance monitoring of each of the thousands of independent reps in the company's downline genealogy. Requirements for such a system include:

- **Incentive Program Time Frame:** Very few incentive programs correspond to the monthly commissions cycle most companies employ. Instead, most incentives span across several months while some last an entire year or more. Most incentives begin and end on odd days. This is often due to convention events, large training meeting schedules, cruise schedules, or some other factor.

- **Overlapping Incentive Programs:** Many companies will often have several incentive programs running concurrently, each with its own set of rules and requirements for the accumulation of points toward the offered rewards. For example, one incentive might focus on earning points toward attending the annual convention while another incentive might be based on a February cruise to the Caribbean. Many reps will earn points toward all incentives. The software must be designed to handle the complexity of multiple incentive programs running concurrently with different rules and requirements.

- **Points Based:** As some incentives correlate with other incentives, earned points must be able to be combined together to earn a reward. Earned points might be redeemed toward hotel costs, airfare, limousine pickup, entrance fees into local attractions, etc. Points might be earned by meeting personal sales volumes requirements during the qualification period, recruitment requirements, or even by assisting your new recruits in their sales quotas. Sometimes points from one incentive can be carried forward to a subsequent incentive program if a reward was not earned or redeemed. Most companies use points to measure the success of an independent rep toward earning a specific reward. This has proven to be the industry's best practice.

- **Redemption of Points:** A mechanism to redeem points for specific rewards is required. Historical information, audit trail of all redemptions, the ability to manually override point calculations (with audit trailing), and the associated views and reports are required.

- **Taxable Earnings:** The IRS requires that the value of awards given for incentive programs must be reported on the annual 1099-MISC form, but only one form can be provided by the company for each independent representative. It is required that the value of redeemed awards (not points earned) be combined with the commissions earnings onto a single form for the tax year. Failure to do this will result in stiff penalties and fines for the company.

- **Parameter-driven:** As incentive programs will frequently change with new ones released from time to time, the company should employ a very flexible system whereby parameters can be defined for a new incentive program rather than writing a new computer program every time a new incentive is desired.

- **Reporting:** Results from the incentives for each independent representative must be available to them on the web and on their commission statement.

- **Audit Trail:** Reps frequently challenge the computation of incentive points and earnings. The company must have a system that provides a detailed audit trail that shows how the points are calculated to defend the accuracy of the point's calculations. Otherwise, the trust and credibility of the company will be in doubt and reps will stop recruiting and selling.

Order Processing—Network Marketing

On the surface, order processing appears to be relatively straightforward. When one truly understands the network marketing industry, however, there are a number of very unique aspects to order processing:

- **Sales Tax:** Network marketing has special rules and laws that govern it in respect to the collection of sales tax. States have universally required network marketing companies to collect the sales tax on behalf of their sales force and submit the collected taxes to each individual state (and sometimes counties). Tax is computed not on the price a rep pays, but on the suggested retail price of the product in anticipation of the rep selling the product to a local customer. Normal order entry systems do not support this complex requirement. With many different sales tax jurisdictions (state, county, city, etc.) in the U.S., this is an onerous task. In addition, the problem is often made even more complex due to the different rules of some states related to taxable and nontaxable products such as food, vitamins, dietary aids, etc.

- **Multiple Payments:** It is common for an independent rep to pay for an order with multiple credit cards because one card has insufficient credit to pay for the entire order. Most order entry systems support only one payment per order. This would not work for a network marketing company.

- **Automatic Recurring Orders:** Many companies with consumable products provide a monthly automatic order service to independent representatives and customers who wish to place a standing order which is shipped monthly.

- **Overpayments and Underpayments:** Many companies accept personal checks as payment for orders. Unfortunately, independent reps often make arithmetic mistakes when calculating the payment due. Often, the payment variances are relatively small, but when multiplied by the hundreds or thousands of independent representatives doing this, the payment total variances can be quite large. Network marketing companies, therefore, usually have the capability to refund overpayments and collect small underpayments from the commissions system.

- **Peak Month-end Volumes:** With most compensation plans based on a monthly cycle, personal sales quotas are often expressed in terms of monthly sales. This monthly requirement results in significantly greater order volumes during the last few days of each month as reps sprint to meet their sales volume requirements. Thus, any software system must support a huge spike in volume at the end of the month.

- **Accounting Issues:** Unique to network marketing is the fact that an order is commissioned regardless of its shipping status. An order placed on March 31st will be commissioned in March, but when it is shipped in April, the company will book the sale as an April sale according to accepted accounting practice. This presents a great challenge to most order-entry and invoicing systems because accounting practices generally would book the commissions in the same month as the sale. This is not possible for network marketing companies.

Order Processing—Party Plan

Party plan companies have special requirements in addition to those listed above. A "party" occurs when an independent rep finds a host willing to invite her friends to her home for a group demonstration of the company's products. The rep coaches the host to maximize attendance and create an optimal selling environment. The host is motivated by the prospect of receiving free or discounted products when she places her own order during the party. The nature of this group experience forces several unique, and often complex, software requirements to be considered:

- **Group Party Orders:** During the party, the independent rep takes orders from each individual guest as well as the host. These orders must be submitted on a group order entry system because they are all linked together. Then the host rewards can be calculated correctly and the appropriate order discount (retail sales profits) can be calculated for the rep. Each guest's name and shipping information must be entered with their corresponding ordered line items. Some companies extend discounts to guests based on their individual purchase volume. This group order with individual guest orders is an extremely unique order entry process that must be designed specifically for the direct selling company. Software that caters to non-direct selling companies would never have such a system designed for order entry and the enhancements would be substantial and costly in virtually all cases.

- **Shipping:** Companies must choose whether to allow shipping of individual guest orders to the guest or to group them together in one shipment to the host or independent rep. The choice usually depends on shipping costs, order fulfillment complexity and costs, and whether the company trusts the host to deliver the products to the guests in a timely manner. Shipping the guest orders to the rep may allow the rep to follow up with guests, but it also adds considerably to the time she must spend on each party. Her costs also increase (gas and car mileage), thus reducing her dollar-per-hour profit which can be very detrimental to retaining reps.

- **Host Credits and Gifts:** When a host has a party, she does so in hopes of receiving various incentive rewards such as discounted or free products. Based on the number of attending guests, the number who ordered, or the total sales volume of the party, various host credits and discounts must be calculated and managed by the computer system. Commissions are usually not paid out on the discounted and free products purchased by the host.

- **Sales Tax:** The company must decide whether to charge sales tax based on the location of the party or the eventual shipping destination of each guest order. For the latter, the complexity of charging different sales tax rates based on the ship-to location for each guest can be quite burdensome for the rep to accurately calculate at the time of the party and submit on her order. If she calculates incorrectly, she may overcharge or undercharge her guests and these inaccuracies may affect the profit she makes on each party.

- **Back Orders:** If two individual guests at a party order the same product but only one item is available, which guest will be shorted? What will you do to satisfy the guest who will not receive the product they ordered? Reps that deal with guest backorders become discouraged and stop selling. Some companies offer vouchers to the guest, in some cases worth more than they purchased, as a credit toward purchasing another item directly. The company may need to allow the guest to purchase a product directly from the company to replace the missing product, as it may be impractical for the guest to attend another party in the future to place their personal order.

- **Individual Guest Orders:** Guests may wish to place individual orders at a later time for additional product, replacement products, etc. The retail profits for such orders should automatically flow to the enrolling rep with her commission check.

Product Returns for Refund

Every product order generates commissions to both the purchaser and his upline sponsors according to the rules of the compensation plan. When part of an order is returned for refund a few months after purchase, a company is faced with the challenge of dealing with the former commissions paid on the order in a previous month. Laws and regulations require a network marketing company to provide no less than a 90 percent refund to an independent rep when they return a product that can be resold.

The company cannot deduct the commissions from the refund. Instead, they must either absorb the cost of the previously paid commissions (which no company wishes to do) or have the software available to calculate precisely how much must be deducted from the reps who originally received commissions. Needless to say, this is a very complex issue. If it is not addressed, the company may be forced to absorb many thousands of dollars in commissions paid on refunded orders.

It is not acceptable to simply calculate negative commissions on the refund by processing a negative volume order. The upline reps who received the commissions on the original order may now receive a different percentage (but this time negative) than what they originally received because of their advancement or demotion in rank or status after the original order was placed. For every network marketing company, this is a significant issue.

Independent Representative Web Access

An independent representative is considered a small home-based business owner. The information an independent rep needs to manage his business, including his downline genealogy, is stored in the company's computer and not in the rep's computer. A rep does not have the capability to track sales and recruitment for other people without access to the company's computer. The company must provide the means for the rep to view the status of each of his downline reps, where they are in relation to the requirements of the compensation plan, whether they have sold any products this month, etc. A comprehensive set of web tools must be made available to the sales force, allowing them to manage their business successfully. These tools include:

- Real-time access to personal and downline status and volumes
- Order entry (individual orders)
- Party plan order entry (for party plan companies)
- Downline genealogy view
- Commissions information and statement
- Incentive points earned and status on incentives

Many companies now offer personal websites to their independent representatives with an integrated order entry system. This allows reps to refer people to their personal website, which is hosted by the company.

Your Requirements Checklist

The most reliable and comprehensive requirement lists are those created by teams of experienced users. Often, the questionnaires and requirement planning documents provided by software providers are helpful in identifying your needs and business rules, as far as the features of the software solution are available. You must assume that if an item is not in the requirements document, it does not exist as a consideration or feature in the software that you are considering. In that case, you must ask enough questions to flesh out your own requirements and determine how well the network marketing or party plan software features will support you.

As you prepare to launch your network marketing or party plan company, we recommend that you begin very early to create your requirements list. If you need one to follow, contact us. It's vital that you tell the software developers what you want and what you require. Don't wait for them to suggest their own ideas. Of course, many have already worked in and around the business of network marketing and party plan, but each enterprise has its own unique requirements.

We have several questionnaires and requirement documents in our archives, one or more of which may be useful to you in developing your own requirements. These tools are included in our LaunchSmart™ System for starting and running a successful network marketing company and party plan enterprise. We would welcome a call or contact to explore how we might assist you in developing your requirements list.

The most comprehensive requirements checklist we have is the LaunchSmart™ Software Requirements System. It takes you step by step through the IT requirements planning for your enterprise, preparing you to negotiate features with your technology and software services provider, define requirements if you build your own solution, and provide the business rules and key decisions that will streamline implementation.

Defining your requirements is a rigorous and difficult exercise, but nothing will compensate for a badly-planned technology launch. Cutting corners will always result in rework at later points in growth. We have learned that growth will break bad systems and fast growth will break them faster. This always results in tremendous slowdown, loss, or even complete failure.

Programmers must know with exactness what you require of the technology tools. The technology and software service providers are amazing in every way, but they all share an important limitation: they do not know the business rules and unique requirements of your business.

With careful and disciplined planning, you will anticipate the most important requirements for getting started and establishing a foundation on which future technology can serve your company's most vital interests.

Technology Vendors

There are some amazing software solutions that have been created over the years that handle the unique requirements of an incentive-driven sales system. You must get your head in the right place before you jump into the technology game. You must select a technology services partner who knows the landscape and who can help you navigate your technology journey. It is very different from buying a plug-and-play software application.

Whether you bring your project in-house, outsource the technology services, or both, the following will help you organize your search for the right provider.

Network Marketing and Party Plan Software Providers

In the increasingly competitive network marketing and party plan software provider market, entrepreneurs and visionaries have several options when it comes to selecting a provider. One search on Google for Network Marketing Software pulled 813,000 results. However, there are probably less than 25 full service providers marketing specifically to network marketing/direct selling/party plan corporations. With all these options in the market, providers are competing for you. With all the price variations and functionality options, you can be selective in your choice. Making the transition from a lower end, less reliable software system to a higher end, full-feature system can be prohibitively costly.

The reality is that only a few providers warrant a closer look. Network marketing software providers are just like network marketing reps; there are many to choose from, but only a few that you can count on to meet your needs and requirements. Those few software providers who will fit your needs are not competing for your business because they can rely on their sound reputations and satisfied client bases to generate new business. In contrast, providers that can't always deliver and have a history of dissatisfied clients are aggressively competing for your business because new business is what keeps them going. Don't make the mistake of equating style with substance. There are a lot of systems out there with a lot of sizzle from appearances, but they just don't work as you anticipate. There are other systems out there that look just plain boring, but their functionally and reliability cannot be questioned.

A reliable full-service provider is a provider that can meet your basic needs with an eye for the expectation of explosive growth. Their system can handle the expected influx of independent representatives and customers to your organization. The biggest killer of a fast-growth network marketing organization comes from not having the proper funding or infrastructure to handle its unanticipated and unexpected explosive growth. Your success can be your death knell. If you're considering a system that can't handle explosive growth with the proper infrastructure, then you're planning your own demise.

Navigating Your Options with Confidence

How do you begin navigating the multitude of options available with at least the confidence that you are looking in the right direction? There are three sources you can turn to. First, you can gain certainty from the provider itself. Second, you can use clients as a good reference point. Third, network marketing/direct selling professional circles can direct your company to some solid providers. These three sources can provide you with the direction you need to select the right provider:

- **The Provider**

  ☐ *Look for Professionalism:* There are a few questions you can ask yourself after you have made initial contact with a prospective provider. Is the provider looking to close a deal or become my technology partner? Are they telling me what I need or asking me what my requirements are? Does their approach to the possible relationship entail a vested interest in my success or a plundering of my pockets? Do they have a track record in adapting their system to my specialized needs and others similarly situated or do they want to modify your existing business model to fit into their system? Do they disclose or conceal their existing clients?

  ☐ *Look for Integrity:* System integrity is essential in areas such as if the custom programmed compensation plan paying out exactly in accordance with the specifications you provided. It should not be altered in any way, shape, or form. And if it is altered in some way, this should be because of the programmers misunderstanding the specifications and should be quickly corrected once they understand exactly what it is you want to achieve. Be very cautious if a provider tells you that they understand your specifications, but they take the liberty of altering the payout because they believe their programmed version is a much better compensation model. This probably means they really don't know how to program your compensation plan nor have the desire to put in the effort and work to program what you want.

Executive integrity is essential in building an early relationship. If they feel your needs are too specialized, or if they are not currently set up to meet your expectations in a timely manner, they should let you know. This should occur at the point of first contact or shortly thereafter. They should not give you false promises and expectations. They should tell you up front if they can meet your current requirements. Providers with integrity will even direct you to a provider who can help when they can't. Any provider of integrity knows that there is too much good business out there to burn a prospect for a few bucks and the cost of a tainted reputation.

> From top to bottom, what holds true for the in-the-trenches rep also holds true for the corporate CEO of a network marketing organization, as well as the service providers to the industry. The foundation of success in professional networking is word of mouth. True networkers are looking to make residual income based on sound relationships, not one-time quick cash. A truly reputable provider is more interested in directing a prospective company to a more appropriate provider than attempting to sign a client knowing they will never be able to fully meet their current requirements. They value the good reputation of integrity and the residual income from new clients. Their reputation will generate more than one-time quick cash.

> *Examine Capabilities:* If you're considering a provider and you question them about their system's capabilities in relation to your specialized requirements and all you hear from them is "yes," should this be a cause for concern? Not

necessarily, it just means they may have vast experience in developing several systems for their clients similar to your company's system. Likewise, when you hear "no" from a prospective provider, this doesn't mean that they can't provide you with an alternative solution already in their system or custom program a solution to meet your requirements. It likely means they did not design their system specifically for your company's specialized requirements. If you engage a provider that has everything you require specifically for your company in terms of specialized requirements, be leery, since it is highly unlikely that they could have anticipated every single requirement of your business.

- ## Clients

    ☐ *Check References:* A provider's clients are your best references. Software providers fall into one of three categories when it comes to sharing their existing clients with prospective new clients. The first category will provide prospects with full disclosure and access to their clients, except of course, for those clients who wish to remain anonymous. The second category tends to be selective as to which clients they make available to their prospects. The third category will not reveal or make available any of their clients.

    A provider that gives full disclosure creates a sense of confidence that they are competent in what they do. It is also a sign that they have satisfied clients and have nothing to hide. It is understandable why a provider may reveal some clients but not all. Less than full disclosure in today's business climate raises questions, but there is often a reasonable basis for limited disclosure. Simply explore this in a healthy, candid dialogue with the provider. When a provider categorically refuses to reveal or make their clients available to their prospects, they often state it is to "protect the privacy of their clients." If this happens, run in the other direction!

- ## Professional Circles

    ☐ *Ask Questions:* Network marketing/direct selling professional circles can assist in finding the best software providers for you if you ask enough of the right questions from the right people. When you do this, a few names always rise to the top. Once you narrow the search to the top three or four, you can then interview them to determine which best fits your company.

Selecting a Provider

Selecting a provider must be addressed with a certain level of importance. Once you choose a software provider, you're committed. If things don't work out, it can be devastating in costs and lost opportunities. You potentially face the vexing situation of finding another provider that can meet your needs and requirements. Remember, you only pay for quality once, so it's worth making quality your first choice.

If you have visions of your multimillion-dollar corporation running on the "off the shelf" software that you purchased for less than $5,000, think again. When you invest in a temporary fix to get you to the next level, your provider perceives your relationship as temporary as well. Because they have no real vested interest in your company's success, and because the relationship is temporary, they are not as concerned with your satisfaction or their product's performance. These types of relationships between a prospective company and a service provider are perfect for the creation of false promises and unmet expectations.

Conclusion

The requirements of a direct selling company are unlike any other business model. We urge you to seek out software providers who are registered supplier members of the Direct Selling Association (DSA) in order to avoid the often costly and frustrating experience of developing software that has previously been developed. DSA supplier companies in many cases have acquired the unique expertise and understanding of these requirements and can often provide a much better product for less money.

Since we do not accept commissions for referring software solutions, you can be sure that we will offer objective advice based on many years working around the various providers. If we can help in the selection, please let us know. The following are our recommended action steps to prepare you for launch.

Essential Action Steps for Launching

☐ Select your network marketing or party plan software

☐ Set up your technology department

Chapter 10
Legal & Regulatory Needs

It's a fact of life: business is regulated. But with the basics in place, a business can confidently launch. Successful start-ups must be well-informed of network marketing legal issues and regulatory demands, so they can navigate the challenging waters of early years.

The law can be a protective wall for your business, and you should diligently close holes and gaps in the wall as they appear. By its nature, the network marketing law protects your company along with its independent representatives and customers by defining and restricting unsavory and illegal practices.

Beware the Legal Pitfalls

Legal issues frequently defy common sense and logic and often remain undiscovered until they have caused serious damage. The passage of time usually compounds their complexity and their consequences, which in turn increases the cost to remedy them.

To avoid these potentially devastating consequences, successful start-ups stay current on legal issues and regulatory demands from the start. Of course, you will want to do everything possible to successfully navigate the legal issues. By knowing the potential pitfalls, you can be more aware of how to aid your company in coping with the challenges before its costs (in terms of dollars and delays) spin out of control.

The most common legal issues that your company could face are related towards compensation plans, products, income claims, consumer protection laws and regulations, and representative agreements and policies.

Compensation Plan

The most common legal problem confronted by direct selling companies has to do with an improperly designed compensation plan. In a worst-case scenario, even if it was designed with the best of intentions, a compensation plan may be an illegal pyramid scheme, which can cause company owners can face criminal charges or even jail time. For example, a marketing and compensation plan that requires independent representatives to make large up-front purchases will likely be viewed by a regulatory or law enforcement agency as an illegal pyramid scheme. This is the case regardless of whether that requirement is explicitly part of the plan or more discreetly promoted by the company or its independent reps.

Likewise, a direct selling program that requires independent representatives to continually purchase the company's products in order to receive a check will be at risk of attack from a regulator.

From a lawyer's point of view, it is necessary that a direct selling company plans and considers how it will generate retail sales. At great risk, start-up companies put their major emphasis into recruiting independent reps and encouraging or requiring reps to load up on products. By developing a direct selling program that is built around retail sales and emphasizing the recruitment of reps, a company can achieve two goals: it can avoid legal and regulatory exposure, and, most importantly, it can increase its sales beyond those made by its reps.

Products

The bottom line is that products must have value. Value is a function of price, quality, and demand for the product or service your company offers. The economic downturn that began in 2008 produced a surge in direct selling companies that produced and delivered products with genuine value. At the same time, the companies that were primarily business opportunities with marginal value in their products experienced dramatic losses and closures. Simply put, they did not deliver enough value for consumers to justify continued consumption of their products and services.

In the end, a question to ask is are the only people purchasing products the company's independent reps? If the answer is yes, are they purchasing products, so they can continue earning commissions or because the products are genuinely valuable?

Because there is minimal to no retail market for low-value products, the only people buying them are independent representatives; this makes it easy for regulators to prove that the program is an illegal pyramid and that the products are merely an attempt by the company to disguise the pyramid. An easy test to determine whether a direct selling company is actually a pyramid scheme is to take a look at the products and ask yourself if you would purchase the products if they were not associated with the compensation plan. If the answer is "no," you are likely looking at a pyramid scheme.

Income Claims

The third legal issue that start-up companies must address is not making or allowing income claims. Income claims come in many different forms including:

- Blatant claims that an independent representative can earn "X" amount of dollars in just two weeks through this program

- Income testimonials by independent representatives

- Photos that present an image and lifestyle of wealth and success— large homes, expensive cars, jewelry, vacations, etc. (such images are considered "lifestyle" income claims)

The problem with income claims and representations is that if the income that is being claimed or represented is not the average amount earned by all of the company's reps, the Federal Trade Commission (FTC) will consider the claim to be unfair and deceptive advertising.

For example, if a rep tells the prospective reps in the audience that he earned $5,000 last month, and even if that claim is one hundred percent true, the FTC and state regulators will assert that the claim is unfair and deceptive advertising unless the average income of all reps last month was $5,000.

The FTC will do everything it can to take down a company that it believes is systematically engaging in abusive practices by making use of inappropriate income claims. This is true even if the claims are being made only by the reps in the field and not directly by the company. The good news is that there are ways to make income representations and claims that do not go against the FTC and state regulators, but they require the assistance of experienced legal counsel.

Consumer Protection Laws and Regulations

The next area confronting start-ups are the countless consumer protection laws and regulations impacting their businesses.

For example, depending on the nature of your products, product labels may need to be reviewed for compliance with other regulations. Dietary supplement, cosmetic, and personal care product labels must be reviewed to ensure that they are compliant with Food and Drug Administration (FDA) regulations. In addition, promotional and advertising materials for those types of products must also be reviewed to ensure that they are not being promoted as prescription or over-the-counter drugs.

Representative Agreements and Policies

Finally, the independent representative agreements and policies between the company and its sales organization require careful attention. Because these documents are contracts that govern the relationship between the company and its reps, they must be drafted with care. To do this, they must take into consideration the company's business philosophies and methods, ensure all relevant issues are addressed, and make sure the agreement is as enforceable as possible.

The LaunchSmart Four P's

Similar to the five pitfalls listed above, ServiceQuest affiliate Steven Richards, from the award-winning firm Grimes & Reese[9] identified four major pitfalls to avoid known as the LaunchSmart Four P's:

- **Compensation Plan**
  - The plan should not:
    - ☐ Promote inventory loading
    - ☐ Front end
    - ☐ Encourage excessive recurring purchases
    - ☐ Pay compensation on recruiting

---

9   Recipients of the DSA 2010 Partnership Award. The firm has since changed ownership and is Reese|Poyfair|Richards at the time this book was released.

- ☐ Primarily reward recruiting
- ☐ Fast start bonuses
- The plan should:
  - ☐ Reward sales to retail customers
  - ☐ Utilize 70 percent and five customer rules
  - ☐ Be 51 percent or more
  - ☐ Deter inventory loading
- **Viable Products**
  - ☐ Available (no pre-selling)
  - ☐ Efficacious
  - ☐ Marketable outside of the distribution network
  - ☐ Price and value
  - ☐ Consumer demand
  - ☐ Training programs
  - ☐ Tool and product bundles
- **Proper Practices**
  - ☐ Independent contractor misconception
  - ☐ Income claims
  - ☐ Unsubstantiated product claims
  - ☐ Deceptive recruiting practices
  - ☐ Returns and refunds
- **Police the Field**
  - ☐ Policy administration and enforcement
  - ☐ Compliance
  - ☐ Proactive field investigation and oversight

Steps to Selecting an Attorney

An attorney or firm that specializes in direct selling will help protect you from making mistakes that will place your business at risk. It is important to become an educated consumer when choosing legal services; however, this process can be confusing if you are not experienced in the field. Here are the best two ways we have found for making the right decision: talk with several attorneys and check your references.

The first thing you should do is talk with several attorneys. You have choices. You should realize is that you have choices. In addition to the ServiceQuest preferred providers, there are other good attorneys who serve direct selling companies. Speak with them, form an opinion, and see how they work with you. We will gladly provide you with the names and telephone numbers of the providers we know of and have worked with since 1988.

The second thing to do is check your references. If you are a network marketer, do what you do best—network! Ask the attorneys you speak with for references. References are the very best resources. If an attorney is unable or unwilling to provide references, recognize this as a red flag.

Once you receive a list of references, be sure to ask about how satisfied they were with the attorney. While the quality of an attorney's work is of utmost importance, it is not the only issue you should inquire about. It is equally important to ask about the referred attorney's responsiveness. Is the attorney generally available? How quickly does the attorney return phone calls? Is the attorney able to promptly respond to emergency situations? There is nothing more frustrating or irritating when your plan is coming together to have it halted for a month or six weeks while the attorney finds time for you.

Be sure to ask your reference about their experience with the law firm's billing practices. Nothing creates friction faster between a client and attorney like surprises on legal bills. So, ask if the client was satisfied with the attorney's billing practices. Were invoices in line with expectations? Were there unanticipated overruns? Did the attorney keep the client apprised of unexpected situations that may lead to increased expenses? Good firms are sensitive to client budgets and strive to ensure that commitments and services are kept within the agreed budgets.

Finally, ask the reference if they have had experience with any of the other attorneys you are considering. Often, a company will have had experience with several attorneys, so they are a good source of comparative information.

The Legal Fundamentals

By taking the right steps at the right time in your new company's development, you can feel assured that your company will be protected. At the earliest stages of your new direct selling business, you must be sure to set in place the important fundamentals listed below:

- Independent representative policies and procedures
- Independent representative agreement and forms
- State registrations
- Legal review of your company's compensation plan
- Legal review of labels and ingredients
- Legal review of literature and promotional materials

Define Your Legal Entity

An important decision you will face is your choice of legal entity. For any type of company, you will need to consider legal, ownership, liability, and income tax implications. Your attorney and accountant can provide essential perspectives.

Corporate Checking Accounts

From the outset, as soon as the legal entity is established, open your business checking account and work with your accountant to set up your chart of accounts, business software (it may be as simple as QuickBooks® for the early months of your business), and tax reporting system.

Intellectual Property

A company's trade secrets are its lifeblood. If this information is not protected, the company's livelihood will be at risk. Various methods (copyrights, trademarks, patents, and other Intellectual Property strategies) will help you to protect your valuable assets. Most direct selling companies sell consumer products and services, making it a highly competitive and very crowded field. It is, therefore, crucial to protect names, marks, symbols, and slogans that help create the unique brand and image that set your company apart from its competition.

Before you select your company and product names, design logos and taglines, print materials, set up your website, and launch your business, you should make sure that you are not infringing on another company's trademarks or service marks. If you do your own trademark searches, start at the U.S. Patent and Trademark Office website at www.uspto.gov. Attorneys with experience in trademarks can also advise you in areas of intellectual property that are not apparent.

The following trademark basics will help to protect you from the very start:

- Use your intended trademark or trade name/service mark in interstate commerce as soon as it is ready and prove its use by documenting the mailing or distribution of materials using the marks.

  ☐ Be sure to establish dates that you first placed the mark into the stream of interstate commerce by noting the date(s) in your records, sending something with a return receipt, etc.

- Use the superscripted or subscripted common law trademark (^{TM}) or service mark (^{SM}) designations to notify the world that you are claiming legal protection for your logo, trade name, tag line, etc.

  ☐ For example, it took us about two years to obtain the trademark registration for ServiceQuest®, so until the registration was awarded, ServiceQuest^{TM} was used.

- Properly budget for trademark/service mark registration work in your starting capital budget.

Sales Tax and Direct Selling

Every direct selling company must be aware of its obligations regarding sales tax. Sales tax, internet transaction taxes, and value-added taxes (VAT) are increasingly hot topics in direct selling. According to ServiceQuest affiliate James Richmond, the following information will help to shorten your sales tax learning curve:

- Network marketing sales tax issues are here to stay. Presently most states impose a sales tax.

- Thousands of local jurisdictions (cities, counties, parishes, etc.) impose a sales tax. Only a few states do not allow local jurisdictions to impose sales tax. Network marketing sales tax is a growing concern.

- Most local jurisdictions are administered by their respective state.

- Some local jurisdictions require a company to have a separate agreement and register if they desire to collect sales taxes in all of the U.S.

- Exemptions vary from state to state. Currently there is no uniform definition of exempt products, services, or entities among the states. Food products are not taxable in several states.

- Food products are subject to sales tax at a reduced rate in some states.

- The responsibility for the collection of sales taxes falls on the retailer. (The definition of "retailer" varies significantly between states and jurisdictions.)

- Some states require all direct selling companies to register, collect, and remit sales taxes and will not knowingly allow the independent sellers to register, collect, and remit. These states are aggressively seeking companies not in compliance.

- The states and jurisdictions that do not require direct selling companies to register, collect, and remit sales taxes have statutory authority to require any company to collect their sales tax if the state or local jurisdiction deems it necessary for the protection and efficient administration of the revenue due, even if that company is not a retailer.

- Some states have "public contracting nexus laws."

- States and local jurisdictions have a vast arsenal of laws that allow them to exercise control over a company for the collection of sales taxes. Companies may rely on Public Law 86-272, which determines when a state or local jurisdiction can collect sales tax. In addition, the company may rely on two constitutional doctrines: Due Process Clause and Commerce Clause.

- The Streamlined Sales Tax Project is an effort created by state governments with input from local governments and the private sector to simplify and modernize sales and use tax collection and administration. There is no specific provision in the project for direct selling companies; however, it will simplify the administration of sales taxes for these companies.

- Companies that retail products directly to the general public or as a convenience to the retail customers of their independent sellers, in addition to selling at wholesale to their independent sellers, will find it more difficult to defend themselves from the responsibility of collecting sales tax than a company that only participates in whole sale.

- Companies that do not collect all the sales tax still have a legal responsibility to ensure that its sellers comply and must obtain a resale certificate from each of its sellers. These must be maintained by the company and renewed periodically.

- While a company may determine that it does not have a legal responsibility to collect all sales tax that are imposed, it may have a moral and ethical responsibility to do so.

- If you choose to voluntarily elect to administer sales tax, do not register without having a formal written agreement with the various state and local jurisdictions.

- Companies that elect to administer all the sales tax will incur some additional costs, including personnel, software, and compliance.

Your company's credibility depends on your knowledge and compliance with the law, your commitment to your sales force and customers, and your awareness of legal and regulatory trends affecting the profession of direct selling.

Companies that do not seriously address the administration of sales tax or ignore the issue altogether[10] may discover that they face significant liability for failure to comply. When it comes to reporting and remitting collected sales tax, your choices will include:

- Manually tracking and completing forms
- Entering data into software that processes and prints forms

---

10   Because laws change frequently, this information can only be viewed as a guide. It does not constitute tax, legal, or other advice from ServiceQuest or its principals or affiliates, all of which individually and collectively assume no responsibility with respect to assessing or advising the reader as to tax, legal, or other consequences arising from the reader's situation.

- Generating tax remittance reports from your direct selling software

- Purchasing sales tax software that integrates with your direct selling software

- Hiring a firm to handle tax reporting and remittance for you

Legal Forms

Your business will use digital and hard copy legal forms depending on the form, software, and web applications you use. Our workshop and workbook, as well as the online resource center, provide the required forms for starting and running your business. We also provide in the Appendix of this guide a partial list of the legal forms available to you, including those that are used the most by start-up and early-stage direct selling companies (see Table 10–1 of the Appendix). We suggest placing a checkmark next to any form you may need for your start-up company.

Independent Rep Agreement Form

The pivotal document in the relationship between a direct selling company and its independent representative is the Representative Agreement. Whether you have a signed original in your files or an electronic signature, the terms of the party plan or network marketing agreement are essential to your company's safety and long-term viability. This essential tool must survive scrutiny in all the states in which your company conducts business. It must withstand the attacks of disgruntled or wayward reps but still invite individuals who would come and be leaders in your company.

Our workshop gives you the checklist and basic outline for designing and analyzing your company's agreement with reps. Here are a few of the key points to consider when creating a Representative Agreement:

- Application/coapplicant information

- Sponsor/enroller information

- Application clause and triggers/web-based enrollment considerations

- Acknowledgment clause

- Rights and obligations of rep
- Independent contractor relationship
- Assignment/transfer
- Ability to amend
- Continuation of rep agreement
- Rep compliance
- Termination
- Breach of agreement/policies
- Anti-waiver clause
- Integration clause
- Unenforceability clause
- Dispute resolution

Policies and Procedures

Rep policies and procedures set the rules of the game for everyone in your business. Start-up companies face three options for creating policies and procedures:

- Hiring a legal services firm to draft policies and procedures
- Writing your own, using a "cut and paste" approach
- Using forms that have been designed to guide the process

Some think they can "cut and paste" their policies and procedures from well-established companies. Without question, you could learn a lot by evaluating their direct selling legal forms; however, creating your own policies and procedures is often a better idea than "borrowing" them from larger companies because they are specific to your company and situation.

Our workshop gives you the checklist to help you design your company's network marketing and party plan field policies and procedures. Here are some key points to consider regarding policies and procedures:

- Definition of terms
- Independent representative ID number

- Development of customers and independent representatives
- Product and income claims
- Products and services
- Multiple distributorships/independent representative benefits
- Trademarks and copyrights
- Transfer, sale, assignment, and succession
- Countries of operation, international marketing, and sponsoring
- Methods for enrolling and renewals
- Advertising and internet
- Literature, sales aids, promotional materials, and web pages
- Media and media inquiries
- Spamming
- Business entities
- Changes
- Commercial sales
- Conflicts of interest
- Cross-sponsoring
- Excess inventory
- Taxes and insurance
- Bonuses and commissions
- Product guarantees, returns, and inventory repurchase
- Dispute resolution
- Ordering, payment, and shipping
- Inactivity and cancellation

Next Steps and Implementation

We know all of this information can be overwhelming, so we provide here two additional lists to help you in taking your next steps and implementing the principles taught in this chapter:

- Next Steps
  - ☐ Learn about your options for legal entities for your business. Consult with your attorney about selecting the best entity before making your decision and filing the appropriate paperwork.
  - ☐ Interview direct selling attorneys and make your selection.
  - ☐ Involve your accountant in setting up the entity, opening checking accounts, setting up accounting software, creating your chart of accounts, and preparing to collect and remit sales tax (including letters of agreement with taxing authorities).
  - ☐ Determine your sales tax collection policies and your sales tax reporting procedures.
  - ☐ Contact ServiceQuest for any help you may need.
- Implementation
  - ☐ Are you currently working with one or more attorneys? If so, list their names.
  - ☐ Is your attorney familiar with direct selling/network marketing laws?
  - ☐ Have you made a decision on the form of legal entity for your business? If yes, what will it be?
  - ☐ If you are not a sole proprietorship, does the legal entity exist yet?
  - ☐ Have you registered your company name with your state?
  - ☐ Have you performed trademark searches on your company name, tagline, and logo?
  - ☐ Have you decided how you will address collection and remittance of sales tax?
  - ☐ Have you established separate checking accounts for your business?
  - ☐ Have you set up your accounting software?
  - ☐ Do you have a Rep Agreement form?
  - ☐ Do you have a sales receipt form for retail customers? If so, does it include the required "cooling off" language?

□ Do you have the business forms in place that you will need?

□ Do you have Rep Policies and Procedures?

To keep up with your legal needs, use the task list (Table 10–2) provided in the Appendix.

Conclusion

With the legal and regulation basics understood, you can move forward with confidence towards launching. At this point there is much to be done. Below are the essential steps to take towards launching your business.

Essential Action Steps for Launching

☐ File registrations in required states

☐ Write your independent representative agreement

☐ Write your independent representative policies and procedures

☐ Set up your legal forms and company forms library

☐ Obtain legal review of your compensation plan

☐ Obtain legal review of labels and literature (including website)

☐ Set up your sales tax collection, reporting, and payment system.

☐ Set up your legal entity

☐ File for protections of your trademarks and intellectual property

☐ Draw up the key protective corporate documents, board minutes, and authorizations

Chapter 11
Money

Money may be the husk of many things but not the kernel. It brings you food, but not appetite; medicine, but not health; acquaintance, but not friends; servants, but not loyalty; days of joy, but not peace or happiness.

~ Henrik Ibsen

Money is in the forefront of the mind of business owners and executives. We talk about money, we think about money, we worry about money. We plan for what we'll do when we have plenty of it, and we reveal our fears, frustrations, and resourcefulness when we don't have enough of it. Why then, with so much focus on money, do so few ever seem to master money? What is it about money that is elusive, complicated, and difficult to control?

In this section, we show you that money does not have to be so elusive. You need to commit to two fundamentals: understanding the relationship between money and your business activities and creating the straightforward money-management tools and strategies in a regular and ongoing fashion.

Much More Than a Money Machine

Some view business in purely financial terms—as nothing more than a way to create money. This approach can work, but it's a very limiting way of doing business. It squeezes the joy out of being a business owner or member of the team that creates the success of the business.

Some are intimidated by the financial side of business and, therefore, avoid financial management. "As long as the bills get paid, I don't worry about finances," is a common disclaimer. This approach might work temporarily, but it is also limiting because it ignores the great potential that lies within the business. Each view remains shortsighted. Both approaches leave something out of the equation. And both diminish the chances of achieving the strategic objective.

Business is about making your life better, not merely paying the bills. The financial view of your business is an essential element of managing a business, but it isn't the only view you should have. The pursuit of money, balanced with the other aspects of achieving your personal purpose and passion, is appropriate and should be one of the most important business objectives. In short, always remember a successful business is the path of your purpose and passion, and finances are a key component to success.

Value, Fuel, and Quantification of Your Business

A business's value is mainly measured by money; however, it is not the only value of your business. Intangibles such as personal satisfaction, freedom, lifestyle, contribution to society, and prominence in the business community also add to your business's value.

Coupled with passion, money is the fuel for your business. Everything either uses or generates money in your business. If your business uses more than it generates, then you don't have a business—at least not for long.

Quantification (the measurement of physical things) is essential to know what results are being produced. Understanding the monetary impact of your business is one of the best methods of quantification at your disposal. Since almost everything your business does involves money, your business is already quantifying itself. All you have to do is record, interpret, and use the financial information to manage your business.

Financial Management System

In order to manage anything (a business, a government, a home, an athletic team) you need to observe what's going on, understand it, make decisions, and enact your decisions.

For your business, your normal business activities (whatever they are, whatever your size, whatever your location, whatever your phase of business) are your sources of information. You need to record the information, organize it, present it so it shows you exactly what is happening, and then use it to make improvements. It's a continuous cycle, as the following diagram illustrates.

Information

Decision making

Figure 11–1: Information cycle.

By expanding quantification into operational and financial sections, the beginning of your financial management system appears as shown below.

Financial info & documentation

Financial reports, analysis, & decision making

Operational info & documentation

Operational reports, analysis, & decision making

Figure 11–2: Information cycle expanded.

Operational quantification measures the non-financial operations in your business. While almost everything has financial effects, there are many other activities that you may want to measure in non-dollar terms (unit sales, hours of work, inventory, turnaround from order to pack-slip to manifesting, etc.). Operational quantification is addressed further in other ServiceQuest® learning systems. Our focus in this book is specifically on financial quantification.

Financial quantification is the collection, organization, and analysis of information about everything that can be measured in dollars. This is collected by tapping into the flow of regular business information—invoices, purchase orders, batch summaries, bank deposits, lease payments—anything showing the movement of money into, out of, and within your business. This information is organized and stored in your accounting system. It becomes useful through various financial statements and managerial reports. This financial quantification becomes the groundwork of your financial management system. See Figure 11–2 for a visual of this cycle.

Components

As you focus on the financial side of your business, you will gain a broader view of the parts needed for your financial management system. It starts with your basic business activities. You should create the documents and information that are collected and organized in an accounting system. Control systems capture this information. Accounting information is then transformed to a variety of reports, each of which has a specific managerial purpose. These reports, as well as your personal observations, feed into your decision-making process. Your decisions shape your business. You can see how the financial management process is an integral part of the business development cycle.

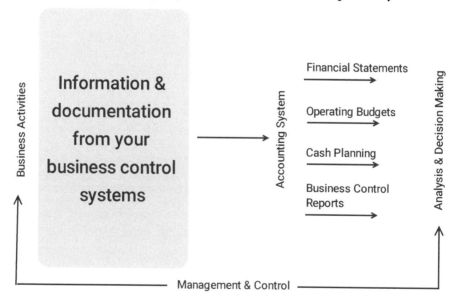

Figure 11–3: Financial Management System.

We will show you how to create or improve your financial management system to take the mystery out of the financial dynamics of business. This won't teach you how to be an accountant—although we provide your accounting team with helpful models for your industry—but it will teach you how to understand the information and advice you get from your accounting team and how to use your team to make better business decisions. It also won't make you into a professional financial analyst, but it will show you how to capture, understand, and use the everyday information to make sound financial decisions.

Most importantly, setting your financial house in order, knowing that you have the ability and tools to control your money—seeing it for what it really is—will set you squarely on the path toward the realization of your goals.

Your Accounting System

As the owner of your business, you know only too well that dealing with the unexpected and the unpredictable is a simple fact of business life. The ability to guide your company through times of uncertainty is a skill well worth cultivating.

But you also know that great leadership requires the ability to control what is in your power to control, to chart a course and set goals your people believe are attainable, and to give people clarity, direction, and security.

Although your accounting system may seem at first glance to be about as interesting as watching grass grow, in reality this discussion may prove to be the backbone of a renewed understanding of one of the most important and fundamental systems in your business. Your accounting system can be, and should be, the place to which you turn and rely on for safety, certainty, and reliability. It's one of your most potent starting points for decision-making and action.

Because your accounting system is made up of those tools and activities that collect data about every financial transaction, your business will benefit from organizing the data in ways that transform the raw data into information. You can then use this information to comply with laws and regulations and quantify the actual results your business produces so that you can make decisions based on reality rather than guesswork.

To address the unique needs of direct selling companies, our workshop and learning system offers an add-in for your accounting system.

Your Accountant Works for You

It's important that you look at your cash flow as an owner and as a manager, not as an accountant. This doesn't make your accountant less valuable, especially since you cannot ignore the tax and regulatory standards. Nonetheless, remember that your financial systems exist primarily as a management tool, then for tax and regulatory purposes.

For all businesses, accounting expertise remains essential—not merely useful, but indispensable. Listen carefully to your accountant's advice, but don't be afraid to ask your accountant any questions you have and explain in detail other available options. Remember, your accountant works for you.

You are the ultimate decision maker, and that's critical. It's surprising how many business owners hand off financial decisions to their accountants because they dislike or are intimidated by "that whole accounting and finance thing." You can and should be the driving force behind the financial decisions and outcomes of your business, with your accountant as an advisor. Cooperation gives you the best results.

Daily Settlement and Processing Systems

The ServiceQuest® Business Process Guide is the source from which we will instruct and implement the daily settlement and processing systems. The activities in the settlement process presuppose the following conditions exist in your company's daily operations:

- Independent reps are being entered into the system
- Inventory is established and kept up-to-date
- Orders are being placed, and payments are collected
- Shipping verification is consistently updated

The settlement processes rely on having independent representative, order, payment, and shipment transactions in place. Transactions are in a state of flux until they reach the end-of-day settlement process. The settlement processes make these transactions permanent.

As you drill into implementation of your daily systems, you will organize your systems into the following essential tasks: pre-settlement, settlement, and post-settlement tasks.

When settlement runs, it primarily deposits cash receipts, updates organizational volume from orders, and posts transactions. These steps are typically automatic when running settlement. Pre-settlement and post-settlement tasks center on the daily settlement in order to ensure accurate results so that you can close the books for the day.

Why do we take time with this rather nitpicky topic? Because the difficulties of launch require that you gain at least a general understanding of how the systems and processes must be designed in order to gain consistency in operations that will support fast growth when it comes to you. This topic is covered in detail in the ServiceQuest® *Business Process Guide*, an add-in to our workshop and learning systems.

Cost of Launching

You may be wondering how much it will cost you to launch. Many variables must be considered to come up with a suitable answer. We'll provide the questions and invite you to supply the answers. We can tell you that some businesses have started with a few thousand dollars and a couple of credit cards, while others have invested millions of dollars in preparations and launch.

Here are some important questions to ponder:

- Are you selling services, products, or a mix of these? What is the status of your services or products? Do they need to be researched and developed? Is the service all set for delivery, or are products in the warehouse ready to go?

- Are you planning to build or lease software to support your business, including genealogies and compensation plan calculations?

- If you plan to hire a consultant, a law firm, a compensation plan design team, or an interim head of sales, what's your budget for these?

- Will you operate from an existing business location, or do you need to secure and prepare office space?
- Will you be filling product orders, and, if so, do you require warehouse and fulfillment systems (regardless of how small or grand)?
- Will your starting workers be unpaid family and friends, or will you be paying your workers money? If you compensate them, how much will you budget for labor costs until the business has cash flow?
- Will you create forms, brochures, and other documents? If so, do you have a budget for creating the templates, writing the copies, and printing them?
- Will you have a starter kit, catalog, or other marketing materials? What is the plan and budget for creating these?
- Will you create a web marketing strategy that includes search engines and social media for presenting your company to the world?
- Do you have equipment that can be used in the business, and if so, what is its value? What equipment will you need to acquire to improve what you already have?
- Will you have a budget for the launch event, travel, and costs associated with the early recruiting efforts?
- What other unique expenses do you expect to have for your company?

Many early worries are solved by completing the launch and operating budget worksheet included in our workshop and action plan. As you work through this important area of planning, don't focus on timing as much as the actual expenses to start selling products and recruiting and supporting reps.

Of course, the purpose of investing money is to increase the invested amount by creating earnings that will repay not only the original amount but also earnings from the money invested and the skill and labor applied. Thus, the earlier your company is open for business, the faster cash will flow to increase (and ultimately replace) the invested capital. And the faster the company operates on its own, without depending on invested money, the faster it can progress toward earning profits. Profits are the essential money rewards that justify all the risks and hard work.

Keeping with business basics, profits are generated when income exceeds expenses. The first important milestone is breakeven, followed by profitability. From our experience over the years we are confident in saying that, as a general rule, start-ups achieve breakeven when they have approximately 500 to 1,000 active reps in the business. This is not the point at which they have repaid the investment, but it is often the point at which the company doesn't require more capital investment.

The pursuit of breakeven and an understanding of positive cash flow are the key financial building blocks for your start-up business. A company may be profitable and yet find itself in trouble if it is not cash flow positive. For example, your company may sell a product that is manufactured in minimum amounts and requires, from the manufacturer, half payment upon placing the order and the other half paid on delivery. If the cash required for inventory is more than what is on hand (which is probable, unless you employ just-in-time manufacturing), the cost of that inventory may exceed the cash that is available from sales in the initial days.

Cost to Continue Operating

Monthly operating requirements will be decided by various factors. Our growth and financial projection models consider several questions; these are the same kind of questions you should consider when setting up a plan and adjusting it once you are in business:

- How many active reps do you expect to have in your very first month of business?
- What percentage of those reps will recruit others, and of those who are recruited, how many will they recruit?
- What will the rep and customer falloff rate be?
- Will your company be engaged in recruiting?
- How much product will customers purchase?
- What will be the consumption patterns and volumes of reps and customers?

- What will you charge for shipping and fulfillment?
- What will your commission payout percentages be?
- What is your product margin multiplier?
- How much will you spend each month to support and grow your business?

The financial model for ongoing operations is available through our workshop, helping you to find out your profitability and cash flow needs. The revenue forecasts that you help to create, along with a capital budget and monthly expense worksheets, will become the financial model specific for your business.

The financial model will prepare you to decide when you will need the money so you can create the disbursement plan to present to lenders and investors.

Sources of Capital

There are two basic types of financing that you can pursue: debt financing and equity financing. Debt financing and equity financing are not mutually exclusive, and, often, a combination of the two provides an option.

Debt financing is an interest-bearing loan, the cost of which has no direct relationship to your sales, profits, or future growth. Instead, the cost of money is determined by the terms of the loan, which are the interest rate and the lifespan of the loan.

Equity financing offers investors an ownership position in your business's future and the right to share part of the profits and final disposition of the assets. Those taking on an equity position will generally require some level of control over the day-to-day operations.

Most start-ups are funded by one or more of the owners. Here are some of the most common sources of capital you can pursue that are often a good match for a network marketing or party plan company:

- **Personal Funds:** This has always been the preferred mode of financing when possible because there are very few strings attached.

- **Friends and Family:** Much like personal funds, these can be good sources of capital. However, there are usually strings attached, even if those strings tie to the annual Thanksgiving dinner table conversations. Be sure to write a contract that clearly spells out the terms and expectations.

- **Internal Financing:** In your business planning and in running your business, don't overlook four important sources of internally generated capital. First, make sure to collect your accounts receivable (your income) as quickly as you can. Second, raise trade credit by seeking out vendors and suppliers who will give you the longest possible payment periods. Third, improve your inventory turnover. Simply stated, inventory that sits in the warehouse is not earning anything and is tying up cash. Inventory that turns over more rapidly ties up less money and generates income more quickly. Fourth, consider leasing versus buying and subcontracting tasks versus doing things in-house.

- **State and Local Development Agencies:** Your state government, local community, and universities may have economic development or business development organizations. These organizations can be an excellent source of information for locally available low-interest loans and even business grants. Sometimes these organizations actually manage their own investment funds.

- **Commercial Bank Loans:** Commercial banks offer several types of loans:

- **Lines of Credit:** The bank makes a certain amount of money available. You withdraw funds as you need them. Interest is generally charged only on the funds drawn. Sometimes the bank requires the line of credit to be periodically paid down or even paid off (for example, once a year) after which the line of credit can be used again.

- **Straight Commercial Loans:** The bank loans money for a period of less than ninety days, after which the complete loan, plus interest, is repaid.

- **Secured Loans:** These loans are made to individuals or companies who give security in the form of real estate, inventory, personal guarantee, or other assets.

- **Character Loans:** The bank loans money for a short term and the loan is unsecured. These loans are generally made only to individuals or companies of high credit standing.

- **SBA-backed Loans:** The United States Small Business Administration (SBA) is an independent agency of the federal government that helps small businesses obtain loans by guaranteeing the loans. There is a fee associated with the SBA guarantee, so it basically increases the cost of capital. However, it's an acceptable path in many instances.

- **Bank Credit Cards:** Although not thought of as such, the bank credit card is a source of funds. Credit cards generally carry relatively high interest rates and should be used only for small amounts of money to be repaid quickly.

- **Term Loans:** A term loan is a business loan with a maturity of no less than one year and usually no more than ten years. Interest rates can be fixed (set for the life of the loan) or variable (tied to some index like U.S. Treasury bills), and payments are made monthly. Sometimes lower monthly payments can be negotiated with a "balloon payment" (paying off a lump sum) at the end of the loan.

- **Private Investors:** You can approach people you know very well, and even those you might not know as well, to invest money in your business. Investors may be passive or active. Passive investors desire less involvement in the day-to-day operations. Active investors desire more involvement in the day-to-day operations. Private investors are almost always equity financers, although sometimes your arrangement with them will also include debt financing.

- **Selling Equity:** Here are some important considerations when you are thinking about selling equity in your business:

  - ☐ An untried, prelaunched business presents greater risk to an investor, who will take a higher percentage in the company to compensate for the higher level of risk. Thus, the cost of selling equity is the most expensive at the beginning of the business life cycle than when the business is operational and proving to be viable.

  - ☐ Investors are investing in you and your ideas, passions, and abilities to make things happen.

- [ ] If investors will have an active role in the business, it's important to define in writing the limits of their authority.

- [ ] If investors will be passive (not actively involved in the business), it's equally important to identify the scope and limits of their decision-making and involvement in the business.

- [ ] The Securities Act of 1933 and the Securities Exchange Act of 1934 regulate the disclosure and reporting requirements for companies offering investment securities. It's important that you are aware of these acts but know that you may be exempt from their registration and reporting requirements. In general terms, if you are not using public solicitation or advertising to market your securities and the purchasers agree to certain things or fall into exemption categories, you may find that you qualify for exemptions that are designed to ease the requirements on small businesses. The best thing is to check with an attorney to see if you are subject to the 504, 505, and 506 rules for exemptions.

- **Sweat Equity:** Partners receiving equity in exchange for expertise, time, and efforts. It's vitally important to discuss and agree upon expectations for the exchange of personal contributions for equity. Instead of granting equity at the beginning, it may be wise to consider the granting of small amounts of equity on a periodic basis (monthly or quarterly) in exchange for time spent in the business. This will give all the parties the needed flexibility for changing circumstances and differing expectations.

- **Angel Investors:** Angel investors are high-worth individuals or investment groups who invest in companies. There are local as well as national angel investor groups that evaluate investment opportunities. A good starting point is to check your local Chamber of Commerce or go online to find these regional business development groups. Much like venture capital investors, angels look for winning combinations of management expertise, Initial Public Offering (IPO), or target acquisition potential backed by strong, credible business plans showing high profit potential.

- **Venture Capital:** Venture capital (VC) firms invest in businesses that appear to have strong potential for later acquisition or initial public offerings. Usually VC firms concentrate on areas in which they hold specialized knowledge or expertise. They look for strong management teams, emerging markets, niche opportunities, and exclusive products that are covered by trade secrets or patents which will give them the advantage. Occasionally, the right firms will also identify promising ventures backed by business plans for high-margin businesses that will generate high returns for their investment. However, VC generally goes into acquiring interests in stable, active businesses. The following list is an abbreviation of high-level concerns of a VC firm interested in investing (a thorough worksheet is available through the LaunchSmart™ workshop):

- ☐ Is the management team of the new business strong and proven?

- ☐ Does the market for the products show a growing trend?

- ☐ Will the products or services be unique from others?

- ☐ Do trade secrets and/or patents protect the products?

- ☐ Is there an exit strategy, or are there companies that are likely candidates to purchase the company in five years?

- ☐ Does the company have a complete, written business plan?

- ☐ Does the business plan make a good case for net profit (EBITDA) of 20 percent or more?

Our limited experience with VC funding tells us that one percent to two percent of companies making presentations to VC firms actually receive funding, and in almost all cases, they give up the controlling interest in exchange.

One unique situation is worth mentioning. We worked with a company that secured four million dollars in VC backing and commitments in exchange for 60 percent ownership and voting control. However, as part of the arrangement, if the company repaid the investment principal in three years or less, they would receive half of the 60 percent given up and the VC firm would retain 30 percent ownership. In just under three years, the company repaid the invested capital in full and won back their controlling interests. This is not a typical situation, but it may help you think about what is possible.

When pursuing any of these sources of funding, a professionally prepared business plan is a critical tool to convince the lender or investor of your credit worthiness. Most will want to thoroughly review your business plan prior to making a lending or investing decision. If possible, try to arrange for an oral presentation to accompany the presentation of your business plan so you can communicate your passion and vision for the business. It is important to realize that many investors and lenders will be initially skeptical of network marketing or party plan concepts and must be educated as to the viability of your business model.

Merchant Accounts

One of the most compelling and universal features of direct selling is that it is a cash business with virtually no receivables. This requires that a transaction be completed immediately, whether payment is accepted by the company over the telephone, online, or in a growing market where network marketing reps and party plan reps accept payments from their recruits and customers.

Accepting credit cards is the key to completing the sale. Instant approvals and customer service are taken for granted, and when payment is declined, the electronic triggers must be accurate and instant. Goodwill flies out the door when inaccuracies or delays come into play.

As you map out your path to merchant account mastery, here is a basic outline of things you can do to prevent issues:

- Contact the participants in the merchant account industry and understand their roles in the process.
- Understand the elements of merchant accounts, how rates and fees are determined, the types of fees that apply, and how the merchant transaction works.
- Understand the process and length of time for establishing a merchant account and gain urgency for starting the application process as early as possible.

In general, businesses that are considered high risk will either be unsuccessful in obtaining merchant accounts or pay substantial fees and high reserves. The businesses and industries that are consistently considered high risk include the following:

- Adult entertainment
- Diet marketers and programs
- Network marketing
- Travel clubs
- Vacation packages
- Telemarketing

For these businesses and other high-risk models to accept credit cards, they typically have to turn to high-risk merchant account providers. These companies are typically offshore, and they always charge higher rates than traditional merchant account providers. Rates can be as high as 20 percent of sales, and some have set-up fees of a thousand dollars or more. The brutal fee structure is to ensure the merchant account providers make enough money to cover the costs of the high number of chargebacks they receive.

Here are six key lessons of what to do be cautious of that we have learned primarily from underwriters:

- When completing the application, avoid trigger words such as network marketing, multi-level marketing, and other wording that would indicate high-risk business.

- Don't get overly aggressive on growth estimates. Slow and steady is best in projections. We have learned that less than $250,000 in a start-up year (typically for an aggregate of six months on a rolling view) stays below the underwriter's radar. Offsetting strategies include multiple merchant accounts and several providers who are familiar with and specialize in direct selling.

- Watch out for memberships and subscriptions that are paid in advance and extend beyond three months. Underwriters do not want the chargeback exposure.

- Be honest. Underwriters dig and investigate. You have a better chance of getting financial backing if you have had problems in the past and you are honest about them than if you pretend there have been no problems and hope they do not discover them.

- Holdbacks (where the merchant account providers hold on to a percentage of collected amounts for a period of time to mitigate their risk) can be managed or possibly eliminated in some instances.

- If you must have a holdback, your target holdback should be between one percent and three percent. Companies with unsavory pasts can expect from five percent to seven percent holdback in the early months and years. The other variable to negotiate is the period of days or months for release of the holdbacks.

Full treatment of merchant accounts is covered in our workshop as well as in our article, "Special Report: Everything You Need to Know about Direct Selling Merchant Accounts."

Your Business Controls

Owning and running a business isn't easy. There's so much that goes on in the course of a day, so many details to take care of, not to mention all the important strategic work such as planning for growth, encouraging field leaders, improving your product or service, and creating a prominent position in your market.

Who has time for the strategic work when you have to worry about the day-to-day details, especially where money is concerned? You will, when you get your business control systems into place!

Business control systems, sometimes referred to as internal controls, are behind the scenes allies that help you move money into, out of, and within your business to the right place at the right time. You may already have some business control systems in place: a system for making bank deposits, a system for ordering office supplies, and a payroll system. If you do, and, if they're working properly, you probably don't pay a lot of attention to them. And you don't need to!

That's the beauty of business control systems. They help your business run smoothly, freeing up yourself and your managers to concentrate on more important matters, and form the information link between your business activities and your accounting system.

On the other hand, if your business control systems could use a tune-up or are not yet in place, you will benefit from the investment of time and energy into getting them working properly. Business control systems are an add-in to our workshop and learning system.

Banking

You need a business bank account. Do not just use the most convenient bank; it may not offer the financial services your direct selling business will demand. Different businesses have different needs. You can interview bank managers in your area by phone to find the best bank.

Using this professional approach will give you an opportunity to establish a relationship with the bank manager. Ordinarily, when you just walk in to open an account, you will deal with the new accounts clerk and never come in close contact with the bank executives. The closer relationship you develop with the bank manager, the better your chances are of obtaining loans and special favors in marginal situations.

Don't be afraid to discuss your difficulties with your banker. No matter how small the problem may be, they may know just how to handle it. Don't pretend to know everything in an effort to impress your bankers. You are an expert in your field, and they are definitely experts in theirs. Learn to talk to bankers in their language, on their terms. It will help your present situation and improve your position the next time you need their services.

In a branch banking state, you will probably do business with a large bank that has many branches. Managers change frequently. Watch for changes and introduce yourself to each new manager to maintain a relationship.

Independent banks without branch offices, or the small chains capable of meeting your needs, will provide the most personalized service. In a small bank, your account may be important; in a large bank, you may never be noticed.

Take time to find the most suitable bank for you and avoid moving your account if at all possible. If you move your account constantly, it will be hard to get a good bank reference to obtain credit from your suppliers.

When opening your business account, the bank will need your Social Security number or your federal tax identification number, your driver's license, and, for partnerships and sole proprietorships, a fictitious name certificate. If you have formed a corporation, bring your corporate seal or articles of organization (for an LLC) as evidence of status. You will need a financial statement when requesting a VISA or MasterCard franchise.

Watch for signs of developing financial problems in your business so you and your banker can deal with them in advance. Plan your growth program and presell your banker. Your chances of obtaining a loan under marginal conditions will improve greatly if you can anticipate your needs and win the confidence of your backers.

Payroll

The key people in your business are employees and independent reps. If you take good care of these people, your business will thrive. Employees perform the necessary operational tasks of the company, and reps drive sales and growth. You will need to pay them, and you will need to carefully follow the laws that regulate working conditions.

Employee payroll and taxes must be instantly set up and carefully monitored for budgetary purposes and withholding tax compliance. Modern accounting software packages such as QuickBooks provide simple solutions, especially for a small business. Most accountants work with QuickBooks and can set up the system from a distance, providing the maximum value to the business relationship while allowing you to manage what you can with staff you bring on board.

Very comprehensive and specific guidance in selecting, training, and developing staff is provided in section nine of our workbook, Operations and Customer Service.

Tax Reporting

Regarding tax reporting, you will be responsible for maintaining records for capital equipment, income, sales tax, and payroll. Keep all records relating to revenues, expenses, and major purchases so you can determine depreciation and amortization expenses for tax purposes. Don't keep records on small items like staplers, digital recorders, and sticky notes, and you won't list leased equipment in equipment records, although you will maintain it under cash disbursements and reflect it in the balance sheet as a liability that is payable each month.

In regard to sales tax, keep the following in mind:

- Decide what your sales tax philosophy will be
- Learn the states that require sales tax collection and take the steps to comply
- Offer to enter into agreements or letters of understanding where possible to mitigate exposure and long-term outcomes

Payroll taxes are essential and must simply become a part of your business. Remember that payroll taxes are so highly protected that even in the event of business failure, the owner of the business becomes personally responsible for unpaid payroll taxes, whether or not they are collected from employees. They are not dischargeable in bankruptcy. Just pay them.

Conclusion

For your business, money isn't everything, but it is a very important part of it. Don't let this part of your company go overlooked. Personally attend to the monetary needs of your company by completing the essential action steps below.

Essential Action Steps for Launching

- ☐ Secure capital to launch your company
- ☐ Obtain your merchant account for credit cards
- ☐ Set up your accounting system, financial, and management reporting system
- ☐ Set up your business controls, daily settlement, and processing systems
- ☐ Set up your company's banking, payroll system, and tax reporting
- ☐ Obtain licenses

Chapter 12
Launch Plan

With all of the things we have covered thus far completed, now you are ready to prepare your launch plan and make the final steps towards the launch of your direct selling business. This final stage will be essential to starting your business strong.

Launch Project Terminology

We recommend the following terminology to help you stay on the same page as us during the planning and launch phases:

- **Prelaunch:** This is the period of preparation and implementation that may include initial founding reps. It is the period that precedes the entry of enrollments and orders, usually because software is being programmed, testing is going on, and bugs are getting worked out.

- **Soft-launch:** When you are satisfied that there are no obvious tweaks required, you cautiously move forward with enrollments and orders, positioning with the field that you are in soft launch. This gives the company an easier "out" (for a very short season) when things may not be working perfectly. It's a true beta test period.

- **Hard-launch:** Commonly supported by a major event to formally launch, this is often strategically timed to coincide with an appropriate season of conferences and conventions (commonly in early January and late August). Oversee contests leading up to this event, promoting enrollments and sales to optimize growth so that the hard-launch finds the company well into momentum.

Keep it Simple, Launch on Time, Stay on Budget

While there are many moving parts in a business, and particularly in getting the business launched, we have learned to encourage simplicity. Perfection is in the process; it's not a destination at which you arrive. Experience has taught that it's far better to start with a simple brochure that is created on time and within budget, then to have the "perfect" brochure. Let your perfect brochure be the one that you create for your immediate needs, with your immediate budget, which can help you get immediate results.

Keep in mind that having a timeline will provide you with many benefits including:

- Allowing you to create a work plan with specific tasks and their assigned periods
- Specifying the dependencies for advancement or completion
- Providing an early detection system for potential delays
- Giving the team a common understanding of status at any given time

In Table 12–1 of the Appendix, we provide a sample project plan that will give you a glance at a project plan with timelines and dependencies, so that you will have an idea of what it should look like and the confidence to create your own.

Depending on your appetite for detail, we have full-featured project plan templates created in Microsoft® Project as well as the simpler Microsoft® Excel. Each has its benefits; the advanced versions simply add more reasonable detail.

Creating the Launch Event

Your launch event is possibly the most important event you will ever hold. It can be the spark that starts a wildfire of momentum. The tasks, and timing of those tasks, associated with the launch event are outlined in the LaunchSmart™ Project Plan. Because of the importance of your launch event, we provide this tool for your use at your company launch event strategy meeting. Below are a few points that will help you consider and organize all the important details that must be addressed.

Event Vision

Define your vision for the event. Clearly state three or four objectives for the event. These objectives will be your guideposts for the event. We believe event objectives should include:

- A firsthand experience with the product/service to build belief and excitement
- A strong belief in the company and its team
- A strong belief in the income opportunity
- Knowing exactly what to do next to build the business

Event Budget and Enrollment Fee

You will need to set an event budget. You might have a target figure going into your planning that will need to be adjusted by the end of your planning.

Budget considerations will include line items under the following groupings:

- Venue
- Participants charge
- Transportation
- Labor
- Show production
- Audio/visual
- Company contributions
- Special meetings and breakfasts/lunches/dinners
- Advertising and promotion
- Gifts and incentives

Event Communication and Advertising Campaign

The purpose of your communication and advertising campaign will be to promote attendance by those who have already joined your field sales force, and to entice others to attend who are still trying to decide if they want to join. With that in mind, determine the major hooks, themes, and messages you will use in your advertising. Be sure that the design of your advertising campaign is consistent with your company image.

At this phase of planning, be sure to consider:

- Prelaunch communications
- "Political" communications such as public relations releases to the Better Business Bureau, city mayor, state governor, company shareholders, key field leaders, etc.
- Types of advertising tools
- Prelaunch newsletters, email drips, and countdown communications
- Prelaunch conference call calendar, with call coordinator and agenda
- Field advisory council (define council charter, establish selection criteria, communicate with the prelaunch council, etc.)

Event Details

A launch event should have:

- **Invitation List:** Determine who will receive special invitations to your event. This could include local dignitaries, celebrity personalities, and important figures associated with your product or service.

- **Agenda:** Go back to your core objectives. Be sure that the event is broken up into small, bite-sized pieces and that the overall pace is fast moving. Spread out "earth shattering announcements" throughout your agenda to raise excitement, and hint at announcements to come later to keep interest and excitement high. Provide plenty of forums for socializing, building new friendships, and rubbing shoulders with key corporate figures and celebrities, and don't plan similar events back to back.

- **Speakers:** Be sure to involve your key "personalities." This includes your corporate icon (the person from the corporate team with whom you want your independent reps to bond), those who can endorse or build credibility for your core offering (product or service), those who can endorse and build excitement around your income-building opportunity, and those who can provide training in successfully building a direct selling home-based business.

- **Signage and Decorations:** Know how you will brand your event. Make sure your signage and decorations are consistent with your corporate branding. Involve your marketing support providers.

- **Venue:** Choose your venue carefully and consider how it fits your company's image. Make it affordable for you. Be sure you have one person as a point of contact for all details, and make sure that the person will be at the entire event. Things will go wrong, and you have to have someone at your elbow to smooth out the challenges.

- **Entertainment and Food:** You will need at least one evening entertainment event. Be sure you choose entertainment that will appeal to most of your attendees. Your food doesn't need to be over the top, but it also cannot detract from the event because it is lacking.

- **Sound and Audiovisual:** Don't cut corners, and don't underestimate the power of music. Use music and lighting to build energy and excitement, to transition between speakers, and to build up important announcements. Be sure to personally screen the subcontractor, whether they are from a third party or part of the venue staff.

- **Transportation:** Consider transportation details that will eliminate the requirement for rental cars. This will keep costs down for attendees and also keep them at your event. Use charter/shuttle bus services and try to keep travel during the event to a minimum.

- **Accommodations:** Be sure to secure special sleeping room rates for attendees. Personally tour the facilities beforehand to make sure they meet your (and your guests') standards for cleanliness and service.

- **Sales:** Determine what products and identity/logo items you will sell. Work out the logistics of processing enrollments and orders.

- **Participant Kits:** Determine what you will include in participant kits. Make sure the kits include some "wow" items and the participants feel appreciated for attending.

- **Event Assignments:** Be sure every element of your event is assigned to someone on your corporate team including planning for the event, monitoring the event, and troubleshooting during the event.

- **Socials:** Carefully plan the social event and treat people as winners. Help them to have a vision of what it will be like when they are contributing millions of dollars of sales through enrollments and the momentum they will create.

- **Uniforms:** Be sure all corporate team members are in uniform or dressed in appropriate company logo-ware so they can be easily identified by participants during the event.

Information Response Systems

The purpose of your Information Response System will be to help answer questions that others may have and to create a voice for the company. They also keep track of updates and changes in the company. They consider incentives to have for enrollments. Basically, they should:

- Identify who will handle company launch calls, both inbound and outbound
- Anticipate the most common inquiries and develop appropriate responses
- Discuss content for company voice mail and hold time scripts
- Develop launch event information on your website
- Develop a launch event "package" to be sent to those inquiring for more information
- Provide training to all who will be communicating directly with the field regarding the event
- Consider fun incentives for securing enrollments to attend (movie/dinner passes, etc.)
- Get an attendance scoreboard up and keep it updated

Practice Makes Perfect

Every presentation should have a "dry run" for approval prior to the event. For those traveling to present, obtain presentation materials early and don't be afraid to ask for revisions. Be sure to have accommodations for last minute changes to presentation materials.

Conclusion

Now that you have reached the end of your preparations for launch, we wish you success in your business and hope we have been of service to you in the launching process.

Complete these last few steps to prepare for the launch of your direct selling business.

Essential Action Steps for Launching

- [ ] Secure capital to launch your company
- [ ] Obtain your merchant account for credit cards
- [ ] Set up your accounting system, financial, and management reporting system
- [ ] Set up your business controls, daily settlement, and processing systems
- [ ] Set up your company's banking, payroll system, and tax reporting
- [ ] Obtain licenses

Appendix
Resources and Tables

Introduction
Additional Resources

- Workshop
- Action Plan

Chapter 1

Table 1–1: Business Plan Table of Contents

Below is the table of contents for a business plan that was successful in obtaining the funding needed.

Table of Contents

Chapter 2

Additional Resources

- RetentionSmarts™ Training Curriculum
- Retention Metrics Workbook

Table 2–1: Council Role and Criteria

Council	Purpose/Role	Selection Criteria
Field Leadership Council	• Advise corporate leadership • Provide a host of high-level services in planning and oversight • Serve as liaison between field and company	• Top producers based on an index (net growth in new leaders advancing in group X increase in volume)
Product Council	• Advise in product training needs and training curriculum • New product or features recommendations	• Credentials (such as medical or research credentials) • Highest average order size in overall group
Training Council	• Oversee field training curriculum • Set up standards and systems for certifying field trainers • Oversee effectiveness of Fast Start System	• Highest producers • Largest average order size • Highest number in auto ship • Training credentials

Retention Council	• Drive field retention through the oversight of retention-based systems	• Highest retention rates in organization • Most productive in enrollments and sales
Senior Executive Council	• Provide stability and represent the attainable • Preside at general/annual functions • Participate as appropriate in planning councils and corporate functions	• Longevity with the company • Maintain senior ranks • Be among the top earners
President's Roundtable	• Represent the dream as an elite, long-term builder • Participate as appropriate in planning councils, recognition events, and corporate functions	• Longevity with the company • Devoid of conflicting loyalties • Capable of holding up to the field as a loyal icon

Table 2–2: Council Sample Agenda 1

Executive Leadership Council Sample Agenda

Tuesday	Guests arrive by 4:00 p.m. at hotel	4:00 p.m.
	Welcome packets in guest's rooms	
	Dinner/social/welcome	6:30 p.m.
	Introductions, light entertainment	
	Overview of council purpose and agenda	
	Close meeting and retire	9:30 p.m.

Wednesday	Light breakfast, coffee, fruit	8:30 a.m.
	Welcome and opening business	9:00 a.m.
	–Recognition of council members	
	–Staff introductions	
	–Ground rules	
	–President's remarks	
	Discuss field leaders' pre-meeting input	9:30 a.m.
	BREAK	11:00 a.m.
	Present and begin council working agenda	11:15 a.m.
	LUNCH	12:30 p.m.
	Resume work session	1:30 p.m.
	BREAK and OFFICE TOUR	3:30 p.m.
	Return to hotel/personal time	5:00 p.m.
	DINNER	6:30 p.m.
	Continue work session/wrap up	9:30 p.m.
	Retire	10:00 p.m.
Thursday	Council departs	

Table 2–3: Council Sample Charter

FIELD ADVISORY COUNCIL

SAMPLE CHARTER

Charter: The BIGCO field advisory council's charter is to advise corporate executives regarding BIGCO strategy and direction, field support, programs, and products. In short, at BIGCO, we want to know how we can improve and we want to stay in constant contact with our field leaders.

Roles and Responsibilities:

- Council Leader
  - ☐ The field advisory council will be led by the director of sales, who reports to the president. The council leader is responsible for:
    - Establishing council member selection criteria and selecting members
    - Establishing council policies and procedures
    - Maintaining open and productive communications with council members
    - Establishing and conducting council conference calls, meetings, and other interactions

- **Advisory Council Members**
  - ☐ Advisory council members will be selected every six months based on performance during the previous six-month period (see selection criteria below). They will serve for a term of six months. Their responsibilities include:
    - Be open and receptive to feedback offered from BIGCO team members not serving on the advisory council
    - Participate in monthly council conference calls and one live meeting per term, as well as ad hoc input as requested
    - Provide open and productive feedback and ideas consistent with the council charter

Selection Criteria:

Council members will be selected every six months based on the following criteria, with numbers being derived from the most recent six-month period:

- Number of new personal recruits
- Number of new members recruited in team
- Number of members in team achieving leadership advancement
- Growth in sales volume in team
- Net member retention: the number of active members at the end

of the previous six months (number of active members at the beginning of the previous six months plus new enrollments)

Each criterion will be evenly weighted and the top 25 members from each country will be selected to participate in their country's respective advisory council. (Note: the top member from each country's advisory council may be asked to participate in a periodic global advisory call or meeting.)

General Activities:

- Advisory council members will participate in a monthly conference call conducted by the council leader.

- Advisory council members will participate in periodic meetings (generally one per six-month term) to be conducted at the BIG-CO home office in their respective country. (Travel expenses—airfare, hotels, and meals—will be paid for by BIGCO)

- On an ad hoc basis, the council leaders may ask for council input in advance of implementation of new products, policies, or programs.

Agendas and Ground Rules:

- Prior to any conference calls or meetings, the council leader will issue a call for agenda items and will issue a final agenda for each call or meeting to all council members. To maintain order and manage time, items not on the agenda at the start of the call or meeting will not be discussed.

- The council will be held to strict adherence to a formal set of ground rules and guiding standards for participation in meetings and representing the council in the field. (Separate document provided.)

Confidentiality:

- All information communicated between the council leader (or anyone else at the BIGCO home offices) and council members is considered strictly confidential. All final announcements will be made from the corporate office.

Decisions:

- BIGCO corporate personal will carefully consider input from council members, after which the corporate team will make final decisions that are deemed to be in the best interest of the entire BIGCO organization.

Conduct:

- All who participate in council activities will maintain the highest standards of professional conduct and communications in all council-related interactions.

Removal:

- BIGCO may remove a council member at any time at its discretion if a council member acts in a manner that is detrimental to the council charter.

Chapter 4

Additional Resources

- Compensation Plan Design Questionnaire
- Introduction to the company, products, and/or business stories
- Testimonials
- Staff training and certification
- Independent representative training and certification
- Independent representative fast start and orientation
- President's message or video newsletter
- Establishing/reinforcing leadership and culture

Table 4–1: Unilevel Compensation Plan

Paid-As Title	Requirements	Compensation						
		L1	L2	L3	L4	L5	L6	L7
Associate (A)	To be determined	5%	5%	-	-	-	-	-
Senior Associate (SA)		5%	5%	5%	-	-	-	-
Associate Manager (AM)		5%	5%	5%	3%	-	-	-
Director (D)		5%	5%	5%	3%	3%	-	-
Senior Director (SD)		5%	5%	5%	3%	3%	3%	-
Executive Director (ED)		5%	5%	5%	3%	3%	3%	3%

L1 = Level one commission   L5 = Level five commission

L2 = Level two commission   L6 = Level six commission

L3 = Level three commission   L7 = Level seven commission

L4 = Level four commission

Table 4–2: Breakaway Compensation Plan 1

Paid-As Title	Requirements	Compensation						
		L1	L2	L3	T	G1	G2	G3
Associate (A)	To be determined	5%	-	-	-	-	-	-
Senior Associate (SA)		10%	5%	-	-	-	-	-
Associate Manager (AM)		15%	10%	5%	5%	-	-	-
Director (D)		20%	15%	10%	5%	5%	-	-
Senior Director (SD)		20%	15%	10%	5%	5%	5%	-
Executive Director (ED)		20%	15%	10%	5%	5%	5%	5%

L1 = Level one commission   G1 = Generation one override

L2 = Level two commission   G2 = Generation two override

L3 = Level three commission   G3 = Generation three override

Launch Smart!

T = Team commission

Table 4–3: Breakaway Compensation Plan 2

Paid-As Title	Requirements	Compensation						
		PS	A	SA	AM	T	G1	G2
Associate (A)	To be determined	5%	-	-	-	-	-	-
Senior Associate (SA)		10%	5%	-	-	-	-	-
Associate Manager (AM)		15%	10%	5%	5%	-	-	-
Director (D)		20%	15%	10%	5%	5%	-	-
Senior Director (SD)		20%	15%	10%	5%	5%	5%	-
Executive Director (ED)		20%	15%	10%	5%	5%	5%	5%

PS = Personal Sales

A = Bonus earned on Associate override

SA = Bonus earned on Senior Associate override

AM = Bonus earned on Associate Manager

T = Team commission

G1 = Generation one

G2 = Generation two

Chapter 6

Additional Resources

- Field Training System
- Principle-centered Training
- Seven Steps to Designing your Field Training System
- ServiceQuest® Field Training System
  - ☐ New Rep Orientation
  - ☐ Compliance Certification

- ☐ Business Skills and Tools
- ☐ Products and Personal Development
- ServiceQuest® Staff Training System
  - ☐ Staff Orientation
  - ☐ Customer Service Skills Training
  - ☐ Advanced Staff Training
  - ☐ Compliance and Policy Administration

Table 6–1: Best Media Usages

Medium	Purpose
Training Systems with Manuals and DVD/CD-ROM	• Orientation (rep/customer) • Basic training • Advanced training systems • Skills training • Audio news features • Convention highlights
Internet and Website	• Web-based interactive training • Company references (forms, brochures, catalogs, price lists, etc.)
Conference Calls	• Announcements • Saturday morning orientation • Business leader communications
Live Training Meetings	• Orientation • Basic training • Advanced training • Motivation • Skills training
Annual Conventions/ Regional Conferences	• Product and program announcements • Inspiration and motivation • Workshops and skills training

Email	• Information
	• Periodic news
	• Advancements
Postal Service	• Newsletters
	• Magazines and publications
	• Product mailers/catalogs/brochures
	• Post cards
Video Mail	• Alternative for conveying some of the same kind of information available through email and conference calls

Chapter 7

Additional Resources

- Business Process Guide
- Business Process Resource Manual—PART I
- Business Process Resource Manual— PART II
- Staffing Plan with Advanced Analysis

Chapter 8

Table 8–1: Staff Resource Efficiencies

- This table presents the results of research done with seven companies, two party plan (PP) and five network marketing companies, which illustrates the staff resource efficiencies (how much revenue the company can produce for each employee on the payroll).

Company	Annual Sales (millions)	In-house Fulfillment	In-house Manufacture	Total Employees	Total Active Independent Reps	Total Customer Service Employees to Total Staff	Customer Service Staff to Active Reps	Annual Sales Per Employee
A	$12	Y	N	28	5,600	7/25%	1: 800	$428,571
B	$25	Y	N	37	17,400	13/35%	1:1338	$675,675
C	$50	Y	N	55	24,500	18/33%	1: 1361	$909,090
D (PP)	$200	Y	N	62	11,600	14/23%	1: 828	$3,225,806
E (PP)	$360	Y	Y	568	54,000	107 /19%	1: 504	$633,802
F	$840	Y	N	1,870	388,000	260/14%	1: 1495	$449,197
G	$870	Y	Y	3,800	725,000	322/8.5%	1: 2251	$228, 947

Chapter 9

Additional Resources

- Web resources with helpful articles and insights on network marketing/party plan technology and software:
  - ☐ www.launchsmart.com
  - ☐ www.servicequest.com
  - ☐ www.mlm.com
  - ☐ www.danjensen-consulting.com
  - ☐ www.mlmlegal.com
  - ☐ www.mlmlaw.com
- Network marketing and party plan software and technology service providers who are members of the DSA (Direct Selling Association), in alphabetical order:

- ☐ ByDesign Technologies, Inc.: www.mlmbydesign.com
- ☐ Data Paradigm: www.dataparadigm.com
- ☐ Directscale: www.directscale.com
- ☐ Exigo: www.exigo.com
- ☐ GSAT: www.gsati.com
- ☐ Icentris: www.icentris.com
- ☐ IDSTC: www.idstc.com
- ☐ InfoTrax: www.infotraxsys.com
- ☐ Jenkon: www.jenkon.com
- ☐ Naxum: www.naxum.com
- ☐ Niche Applications, Inc.: www.inpowersuite.com
- ☐ Party Plan Solutions: www.partyplansolutions.com
- ☐ Software Design of Kentucky: www.sdkdirect.com
- ☐ Thatcher Technology Group, LLC: www.thatchertech.com
- ☐ Trinity Software: www.trinitysoft.net
- ☐ Zoyto: www.zoyto.com

Chapter 10

Advanced Resources

- White Paper: "State and Local Sales Tax: What Direct Sellers Need to Know"
- White Paper: "Legal Principles of Direct Selling"
- Comprehensive Due Diligence Checklist (fee)
- Model Letter of Understanding with Instructions (fee)
- State Registration System with Instructions (fee)
- Model Rep Agreement (fee)
- Model Policies and Procedures (fee)

Table 10–1: Legal Forms

Form	Purpose
Independent Representative Agreement	Enrolling a new rep
Preferred Customer Agreement	Enrolling a new preferred customer
Rep Order Form/Customer Order Form	Ordering products
Retail Customer Order Form	Placing an order for a retail customer
Host Reward Form	Tracking/Computing Host Reward
Auto ship Authorization Form	Establishing a recurring order
Auto ship Cancellation Form	Requesting cancellation of auto ship order
Account Update Form	Updating information on account
Guest Order Form	Guest order at a home party
Host Order Form	Host credits and rewards for hosting home party
Home Party Recap Form	Summary of orders placed at a home party
Supply Order Form	Ordering business aids and supplies
Return Authorization Form	Requesting authorization to return or exchange products
Business Entity Registration Form	Registering a business entity as an independent rep
Rep Cancellation Form	Control form for processing rep account cancellation
Correction of Enroller Authorization Form	Obtaining authorizations to correct enroller on account
Correction of Enroller Request Form	Requesting enroller correction
Federal ID Form	Gathering tax information from rep for account

Organization Change Authorization Form	Obtaining authorization to change organization placement
Organization Change Request Form	Requesting change of organization placement
Sale of Organization Authorization Form	Obtaining authorization to sell business organization
Sale of Organization Request Form	Requesting authorization to sell/transfer organization

Table 10–2: Legal Task List

✓	Task List
Define Legal Needs	
	Start-up Service
	Entity Selection and Formation
	Product Packaging and Labeling Review
	Literature/Copy Review
	Business Kit Review
	Intellectual Property Protections
Legal Filings, Reviews, and Registrations	
	General Business, Local, Warehousing, Zoning
	Importer
	State Tax ID Number(s)
	Federal Tax ID Number(s)
	Non-prescription Drug Applications
	Hazardous Product Submittals
	Surety Bonds
	Sales Tax and Voluntary Compliance
	Intellectual Property Filings and Registrations
	Corporate Registrations
	Business Opportunity Registrations
	Anti-pyramid Registrations

	Direct Selling Registrations
	Employment Planning and Compliance
Independent Rep Forms and Agreements	
	Application and Rep Agreement
	Auto ship Authorization Provision/Form
	FTC "Cooling Off" Documentation
	Compensation Plan Review
	Policies and Procedures
	Contracts and Lease Requirements
	Parcel Delivery Services
	Customs Brokerage Services
	Equipment and Facility Leases/Purchases

Chapter 12

Additional Resources Available to ServiceQuest® Clients

- Launch Event Checklist and Planner (WORD)
- Launch Project Task List and Timeline (EXCEL)
- Launch Project Task List and Timeline (PROJECT)
- Launch Project Task List and Timeline with International (EXCEL and PROJECT)

Table 12–1: Launch Project Plan Sample

Snapshot of Launch Project Plan created in Microsoft® Project.

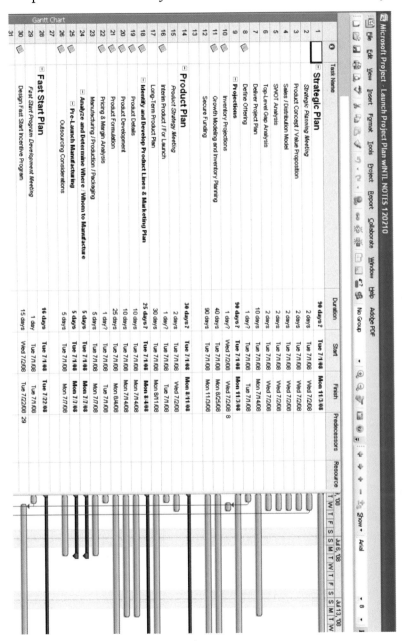

Made in the USA
Columbia, SC
21 December 2019